R. Gupta's®

THE MAGIC OF
VEDIC
Mathematics

Simple Steps to Make Mental Calculation Easier

by

MAYANK GARG
&
RPH EDITORIAL BOARD

Ramesh Publishing House, New Delhi

Published by
O.P. Gupta *for* Ramesh Publishing House

Admin. Office
12-H, New Daryaganj Road, Opp. Officers' Mess,
New Delhi-110002 ✆ 23261567, 23275224, 23275124

E-mail: info@rameshpublishinghouse.com
Website: www.rameshpublishinghouse.com

Showroom
● Balaji Market, Nai Sarak, Delhi-6 ✆ 23253720, 23282525
● 4457, Nai Sarak, Delhi-6, ✆ 23918938

Book Code: R-1718

ISBN: 978-93-5012-503-8

4th Edition: 1805

HSN Code: 49011010

Contents

ACKNOWLEDGEMENT

"All your dreams can come true if you have the courage to pursue them."

–Walt Disney

This book would have been a distant dream if Mr. Sanjiv Pandey & Mr. Vaibhav Pande had not motivated me to take the first step towards writing this book. I am grateful to my parents, Mr. Manoj Kumar Garg & Mrs. Sangeeta Garg, who have made me whatever I am today. I would like to thank my sister Neha Garg, who has always supported me in every possible way.

I would like to thank my relatives and friends for their continuous support and guidance. A special thanks to Ritu Pande, Rohit Garg, Ratika Garg, Anshul Vashisht, Anupam Pande, Akanksha Farswan, Nitish Bhatt, Nitin Rawat, Ashish Gupta, Amrat Bansal, Jitesh Da & Ayushi Pandey.

At last but not the least, I would like to thank teachers and management of Beersheba School, Haldwani and Uttaranchal University (UIT), Dehradun for helping me in achieving whatever I have achieved.

THE MAGIC OF
VEDIC
Mathematics

CHECK YOUR SPEED AND ACCURACY

"Until you value yourself, you won't value your time. Until you value your time, you will not do anything with it."

By : M. Scott Peck

Time Taken : _________

Solve the following questions:

1.   9 3
     8 7

  Ans. _________

2.   9 6
    1 0 9

  Ans. _________

3.   7 8 6
    5 2 1

  Ans. _________

4.   3 4 9
    7 8 1

  Ans. _________

5.   2 1 3 4   **6.**   7 1 2 1
                8 3 4 7   1 2 8 3

Ans. __________   Ans. __________

Find the Squares of the following questions:

7.   89   **8.**   73

Ans. __________   Ans. __________

9.   56   **10.**   65

Ans. __________   Ans. __________

11.   41   **12.**   94

Ans. __________   Ans. __________

Find the Cubes of the following questions:

13.   31   **14.**   62

Ans. __________   Ans. __________

15. 92

Ans. _________

16. 83

Ans. _________

17. 45

Ans. _________

18. 22

Ans. _________

Find the Square Root of the following questions:

19. 841

Ans. _________

20. 1296

Ans. _________

21. 4761

Ans. _________

22. 6561

Ans. _________

23. 8649

Ans. _________

24. 9025

Ans. _________

Find the Cube Roots of the following questions:

25. 9261

Ans. _________

26. 54872

Ans. _________

27.   68921   **28.**   238328

          Ans. __________   Ans. __________

29.   531441   **30.**   778688

          Ans. __________   Ans. __________

Solve the following Questions:

31.   987/3   **32.**   11389/7

          Ans. __________   Ans. __________

33.   296586/6   **34.**   963852/4

          Ans. __________   Ans. __________

35.   989757/9   **36.**   654832/8

          Ans. __________   Ans. __________

INTRODUCTION

Vedic Mathematics is the name given to the ancient system of mathematics which was used by people to calculate the problems of mathematics mentally and with fast speed. Some people may wonder why it is called "Vedic". This is so because its roots lie in the Vedas which were written between 1500 – 900 BCE. Vedas are ancient Indian texts which contain knowledge about various fields like Science, Mathematics etc. Vedic Mathematics is based on one of the 4 Vedas, i.e., on the Atharvaveda. This system is based on 16 Sutras by which any Mathematical problem can be solved.

The whole credit of rediscovering Vedic Mathematics from the ancient Indian Scriptures goes to Late Shri Bharati Krishna Tirthaji (1884–1960). He was a great scholar of Sanskrit, Mathematics, History and Philosophy. Apart from this he was also the former Shankaracharya of Puri, India. He studied these ancient texts for years and came out with 16 volumes of work. But somehow all these were lost and in his final years he wrote a single volume, which was published 5 years after his death.

Late Shri Bharati Krishna Tirthaji

Everyone is looking for new ways of solving mathematical problems and that is the main reason behind the interest in Vedic Mathematics. These Sutras are easy to apply and they cover each and every part of Mathematics. No doubt there are many advantages of using these Sutras like these are easy to apply, more efficient, flexible and fast as you can solve most of the questions mentally. These Sutras not only induce creativity in intelligent students but can also help slow learners in understanding mathematics.

From the last few years, there are various organizations in India and abroad that are promoting Vedic Mathematics. Today, Vedic Mathematics is not only taught in Schools but it is even taught in Engineering and Management colleges. Even students of IITs are said to be using this ancient technique for quick calculations. No wonder why Dr. Murli Manohar Joshi, former Union Minister for Science and Technology stressed upon the significance of Vedic Mathematics.

VEDIC SUTRAS AND SUB-SUTRAS

16 VEDIC SUTRAS

1. Ekadhikena Purvena (एकाधिकेन पूर्वेण)

2. Nikhilam Navatascharamam Dasatah (निखिलं नवतश्चरमं दशतः)

3. Urdhva Tiryagbhyam (ऊर्ध्वतिर्यग्भ्याम्)

4. Paravartya Yojayet (परावर्त्य योजयेत्)

5. Sunyam Samya Samuchaye (शून्यं साम्यसमुच्चये)

6. Anurupye Sunyamanyat ((आनुरूप्ये) शून्यमन्यत्)

7. Sankalana–Vyavakalanabhyam (also a corollary) (संकलनव्यवकलनाभ्याम्)

8. Puranapuranabhyam (पूरणापूरणाभ्याम्)

9. Chalanakalanabhyam (चलनकलनाभ्याम्)

10. Yavadunam (यावदूनम्)

11. Vyastisamastih (व्यष्टिसमष्टिः)

12. Sesanyankena Charamena (शेषाण्यङ्केन चरमेण)

13. Sopantya Dvayamantyam (सोपान्त्यद्वयमन्त्यम्)

14. Ekanyunena Purvena (एकन्यूनेन पूर्वेण)

15. Gunita Samuchyah (गुणितसमुच्चयः)

16. Gunaka Samuchyah (गुणकसमुच्चयः)

13 SUB - SUTRAS

1. Anurupyena (आनुरूप्येण)

2. Sisyate Sesasamjnah (शिष्यते शेषसंज्ञः)

3. Adyamadyenantya-mantyena (आद्यमाद्येनान्त्यमन्त्येन)

4. Kevalaih Saptakam Gunyat (केवलैः सप्तकं गुण्यात्)

5. Vestanam (वेष्टनम्)

6. Yavadunam Tavadunam (यावदूनं तावदूनम्)

7. Yavadunam Tavadunikrtya Varganca Yojayet (यावदूनं तावदूनीकृत्य वर्गं च योजयेत्)

8. Antyayordasake'pi (अन्त्ययोर्दशकेऽपि)

9. Antyayoreva (अन्त्ययोरेव)

10. Samuchyayagunitah (समुच्चयगुणितः)

11. Lopanasthapanabhyam (लोपस्थापनाभ्याम्)

12. Vilokanam (विलोकनम्)

13. Gunitasamuchyay Samuchyayagunitah (गुणितसमुच्चयः समुच्चयगुणितः)

In the text, the words Sutra, aphorism, formula are used synonymously. So are also the words Upa-sutra, Sub-sutra, Sub-formula, corollary used.

Some importants Sutras and Sub-Sutras are explained below with few examples to understand how they work and make mathematics easier.

I. Ekadhikena Purvena

The Sutra Ekadhikena Purvena means: "By one more than the previous one".

(i) Squares of numbers ending in 5 :

Now we relate the sutra to the 'squaring of numbers ending in 5'. Consider the example 15^2.

Here the number is 15. We have to find out the square of the number. For the number 15, the last digit is 5 and the 'previous' digit is 1. Hence, 'one more than the previous one', that is, $1 + 1 = 2$. The Sutra, gives the procedure 'to multiply the previous digit 1 by one more than itself, that is, by 2'. It becomes the L.H.S (left hand side) of the result, that is, $1 \times 2 = 2$. The R.H.S (right hand side) of the result is 5^2, that is, 25.

Thus $\quad\quad 15^2 = 1 \times 2 / 25 = 225$.

Similarly,

$$25^2 = 2 \times (2 + 1)/25 = 2 \times 3/25 = 625;$$
$$35^2 = 3 \times (3 + 1)/25 = 3 \times 4/25 = 1225;$$
$$45^2 = 4 \times (4 + 1)/25 = 4 \times 5/25 = 2025;$$
$$65^2 = 6 \times 7/25 = 4225;$$
$$105^2 = 10 \times 11/25 = 11025;$$
$$135^2 = 13 \times 14/25 = 18225;$$

(ii) Vulgar fractions with denominators ending in 9:

We now take examples of $1/n9$, where $n = 1, 2, \text{———}, 9$. In the conversion of such vulgar fractions into recurring decimals, Ekadhika process can be effectively used both in division and multiplication.

(a) Division Method : Value of 1/19.

The numbers of decimal places before repetition is the difference of numerator and denominator, *i.e.*, $19 - 1 = 18$ places.

For the denominator 19, the *purva* (previous) is 1.

Hence, *Ekadhikena purva* (one more than the previous) is $1 + 1 = 2$.

The method of division is as follows:

Step. 1 : Firstly, We divide numerator 1 by 20.

$\quad\quad\quad$ *i.e.*, $1/20 = 0.1/2 = {}_{.1}0$ (0 times, 1 remainder)

Step. 2 : We divide 10 by 2.

$\quad\quad\quad$ *i.e.*, 0.0_05 (5 times, 0 remainder)

Step. 3 : We divide 5 by 2

$\quad\quad\quad$ *i.e.*, 0.05_12 (2 times, 1 remainder)

Step. 4 : We divide ${}_1 2$ *i.e.*, 12 by 2

$\quad\quad\quad$ *i.e.*, 0.0526 (6 times, No remainder)

Step. 5 :   We divide 6 by 2

 i.e., 0.05263 (3 times, No remainder)

Step. 6 :   We divide 3 by 2

 i.e., 0.05263_11 (1 time, 1 remainder)

Step. 7 :   We divide $_11$ *i.e.,* 11 by 2

 i.e., 0.052631_15 (5 times, 1 remainder)

Step. 8 :   We divide $_15$ i.e., 15 by 2

 i.e., 0.0526315_17 (7 times, 1 remainder)

Step. 9 :   We divide $_17$ *i.e.,* 17 by 2

 i.e., $0.05263157\,_18$ (8 times, 1 remainder)

Step. 10 :   We divide $_18$ *i.e.,* 18 by 2

 i.e., 0.0526315789 (9 times, No remainder)

Step. 11 :   We divide 9 by 2

 i.e., $0.0526315789\,_14$ (4 times, 1 remainder)

Step. 12 :   We divide $_14$ *i.e.,* 14 by 2

 i.e., 0.052631578947 (7 times, No remainder)

Step. 13 :   We divide 7 by 2

 i.e.,, 0.052631578947_13 (3 times, 1 remainder)

Step. 14 :   We divide $_13$ *i.e.,* 13 by 2

 i.e., 0.0526315789473_16 (6 times, 1 remainder)

Step. 15 :   We divide $_16$ *i.e.,* 16 by 2

 i.e., 0.052631578947368 (8 times, No remainder)

Step. 16 :   We divide 8 by 2

 i.e.,, 0.0526315789473684 (4 times, No remainder)

Step. 17 :   We divide 4 by 2

 i.e., 0.05263157894736842 (2 times, No remainder)

Step. 18 :   We divide 2 by 2

 i.e., 0.052631578947368421 (1 time, No remainder)

Now from step 19, *i.e.,* dividing 1 by 2, Step 2 to Step 18 repeats thus giving

$$\overline{1/19 = 0.052631578947368421} \text{ or } 0.0\overset{\bullet}{5}2631578947368421\overset{\bullet}{}$$

It is interesting to note that we have completed the process of division only by using '2'. Nowhere the division by 19 occurs.

(b) Multiplication Method: Value of 1/19

For a fraction of the form in whose denominator 9 is the last digit, we take the case of 1/19 as follows:

For 1/19, 'previous' of 19 is 1. And one more than of it is 1 + 1 = 2.

Therefore 2 is the multiplier for the conversion. We write the last digit in the numerator as 1 and follow the steps leftwards.

Step. 1 :   1

Step. 2 :   21(multiply 1 by 2, put to left)

Step. 3 :   421(multiply 2 by 2, put to left)

Step. 4 :   8421(multiply 4 by 2, put to left)

Step. 5 : $_1$68421 (multiply 8 by 2 =16, 1 carried over, 6 put to left)

Step. 6 : $_1$368421 (6 × 2 =12, +1 [carry over]

         = 13, 1 carried over, 3 put to left)

Step. 7 :   7368421 (3 × 2, = 6 +1 [carry over] = 7, put to left)

Step. 8 : $_1$47368421 (as in the same process)

Step. 9 :   947368421 (Do – continue to step 18)

Step. 10 : $_1$8947368421

Step. 11 : $_1$78947368421

Step. 12 : $_1$578947368421

Step. 13 : $_1$1578947368421

Step. 14 :   31578947368421

Step. 15 :   631578947368421

Step. 16 : $_1$2631578947368421

Step. 17 :   52631578947368421

Step. 18 :   1052631578947368421

Now from step 18 onwards the same numbers and order towards left continue.

Thus **1/19 = 0.052631578947368421**

Note that we have

(i) not at all used division process

(ii) instead of dividing 1 by 19 continuously, just multiplied 1 by 2 and continued to multiply the resultant successively by 2 till the desired answer.

2. Nikhilam Navatascaramam Dasatah

Simply the formula means : "all from 9 and the last from 10"

The formula can be applied in multiplication of numbers, which are nearer to bases like 10, 100, 1000 *i.e.*, to the powers of 10. The procedure of multiplication using the Nikhilam involves minimum number of steps, space, time saving and only mental calculation. The numbers taken can be either less or more than the base considered.

The difference between the number and the base is termed as deviation which may be positive or negative. Positive deviation is written without the positive sign and the negative deviation, is written using Rekhank (a bar on the number). Now observe the following table.

Number	Base	Number – Base	Deviation
16	10	16 – 10	6
7	10	7 – 10	–3 or $\bar{3}$
98	100	98 – 100	–02 or $\overline{02}$
112	100	112 – 100	12
993	1000	993 – 1000	–007 or $\overline{007}$
1011	1000	1011 – 1000	011

Some rules of the method (near to the base) in Multiplication

(a) Since deviation is obtained by Nikhilam sutra we call the method as Nikhilam multiplication.

   Eg : 94. Now deviation can be obtained by 'all from 9 and the last from 10' sutra *i.e.*, the last digit 4 is from 10 and remaining digit 9 from 9 gives 06.

(b) The two numbers under consideration are written one below the other. The deviations are written on the right hand side.

Eg : Multiply 7 by 8.

Now the base is 10. Since it is near to both the numbers, we write the numbers one below the other.
$$7$$
$$8$$

Take the deviations of both the numbers from the base and represent
$$7\ \bar{3}$$
$$8\ \bar{2}$$

Rekhank or the minus sign before the deviations

or
$$7 - 3$$
$$8 - 2$$

or remainders 3 and 2 implies that the numbers to be multiplied are both less than 10

(c) The product or answer will have two parts, one on the left side and the other on the right. A vertical or a slant line (*i.e.*, a slash) may be drawn for the demarcation of the two parts *i.e.*,

$$\begin{matrix} 7 & \bar{3} \\ 8 & \bar{2} \end{matrix} \Big/ \qquad \text{(or)} \qquad \begin{matrix} 7 & -3 \\ 8 & -2 \end{matrix} \Big/$$

(d) The R.H.S. of the answer is the product of the deviations of the numbers. It shall contain the number of digits equal to number of zeroes in the base.

$$i.e., \quad \begin{matrix} 7 & \bar{3} \\ 8 & \bar{2} \end{matrix}$$
$$/ \ (3 \times 2) = 6$$

Since base is 10, 6 can be taken as it is.

(e) L.H.S of the answer is the sum of one number with the deviation of the other. It can be arrived at in any one of the four ways.

(i) Cross-subtract deviation 2 on the second row from the original number 7 in the first row *i.e.*, $7 - 2 = 5$.

(ii) Cross.subtract deviation 3 on the first row from the original number 8 in the second row (converse way of (i))

  i.e., 8 − 3 = 5

(iii) Subtract the base 10 from the sum of the given numbers.

  i.e., (7 + 8) − 10 = 5

(iv) Subtract the sum of the two deviations from the base.

  i.e., 10 − (3 + 2) = 5

Hence, 5 is left hand side of the answer.

$$\text{Thus} \quad \begin{array}{cc} 7 & \bar{3} \\ 8 & \bar{2} \\ \hline 5/ & \end{array}$$

Now (d) and (e) together give the solution

$$\begin{array}{cc} 7 & \bar{3} \\ 8 & \bar{2} \\ \hline 5 & / \ 6 \end{array} \quad i.e., \quad \begin{array}{r} 7 \\ \times \ 8 \\ \hline 56 \end{array}$$

(f) If R.H.S. contains less number of digits than the number of zeros in the base, the remaining digits are filled up by giving zero or zeroes on the left side of the R.H.S. If the number of digits are more than the number of zeroes in the base, the excess digit or digits are to be added to L.H.S of the answer.

The general form of the multiplication under Nikhilam can be shown as follows:

Let N_1 and N_2 be two numbers near to a given base in powers of 10, and D_1 and D_2 are their respective deviations from the base. Then $N_1 \times N_2$ can be represented as

$$\begin{array}{cc} N_1 & D_1 \\ N_2 & D_2 \\ \hline (N_1 + D_2) \text{ or} & \Big/ \ D_1 \times D_2 \\ (N_2 + D_1) & \Big/ \end{array}$$

Case (i) : When both the numbers are lower than the base.

Ex. 1: Find 97 × 94. Here base is 100. Following the rules, the working is as follows:

$$
\begin{array}{cc}
97 & \overline{03} \\
94 & \overline{06} \\
\hline
(97-06)\text{ or} & /\ 3\times 6 \\
(94-03) & /\ = 9118
\end{array}
$$

Ex. 2: 75 × 95. Base is 100.

$$
\begin{array}{cc}
75 & \overline{25} \\
95 & \overline{05} \\
\hline
(75-05)\text{ or} & /\ 25\times 5 = 70/\ _1 25 \text{ (observe rule-f)} \\
(95-25) & /\qquad = (70+1)/25 = 7125
\end{array}
$$

Ex. 3: 994 × 988. Base is 1000.

$$
\begin{array}{cc}
994 & \overline{006} \\
988 & \overline{012} \\
\hline
(994-12)\text{ or} & /\ 6\times 12 = 982/072 \text{ (rule-f)} \\
(988-06) & /\qquad = 982072
\end{array}
$$

Case (ii) : When both the numbers are higher than the base.

The method and rules follow as they are. The only difference is the positive deviation. Instead of cross – subtract, we follow cross – add.

Ex. 4: 18 × 14. Base is 10.

$$
\begin{array}{cc}
18 & 08 \\
14 & 04 \\
\hline
(18+12)\text{ or} & /\ 8\times 4 = 22/\ _3 2 \text{ (rule-f, 3 carry over)} \\
(14-03) & /\qquad = 252
\end{array}
$$

Ex. 5: 104 × 102. Base is 100.

$$104 \quad 04$$
$$102 \quad 02$$
$$\overline{106 \,/\, 4 \times 2} = 10608 \text{ (rule-f)}$$

Ex. 6: 1275 × 1004. Base is 1000.

$$1275 \quad 275$$
$$1004 \quad 004$$
$$\overline{1279/275 \times 4} = 1279/_1 100 \text{ (rule-f)}$$
$$= 1280100$$

Case (iii): When one number is more and the other is less than the base.

In this situation one deviation is positive and the other is negative. So the product of deviations becomes negative. So the right hand side of the answer obtained will therefore have to be subtracted. To have a clear representation and understanding a vinculum is used. It proceeds into normalization.

Ex.7: 13 × 7. Base is 10

$$13 \qquad 03$$
$$7 \qquad \overline{03}$$
$$\overline{\begin{array}{c}(13-03) \text{ or} \\ (7+03)\end{array}} \Big/ \, 3 \times \overline{3} = 10/\overline{9} = 100 - 9 = 91$$

Ex. 8: 108 × 94. Base is 100.

$$108 \qquad 08$$
$$94 \qquad \overline{06}$$
$$\overline{\begin{array}{c}(108-06) \text{ or} \\ (94+08)\end{array}} \Big/ \, 8 \times \overline{6} = 102/\overline{48} = 10152 \text{ (Since the complement of 48 is 52 - base 10)}$$

Ex. 9: 998 × 1025. Base is 1000.

$$998 \qquad \overline{002}$$

$$1025 \qquad \overline{025}$$

$$\frac{(998-25) \text{ or}}{(1025+2)} \Big/ \overline{2} \times 25 = 1023/\overline{050} = 1022950 \text{ (Since the}$$
complement of 50 is 950 for the base 1000)

3. Urdhva-tiryagbhyam

Urdhva – tiryagbhyam is the general formula applicable to all cases of multiplication and also in the division of a large number by another large number. It means

(a) Multiplication of two 2 digit numbers.

Ex. 1: Find the product 14 × 12

(i) The right hand most digit of the multiplicand, the first number (14) *i.e.*,4 is multiplied by the right hand most digit of the multiplier, the second number (12) *i.e.*, 2. The product 4 × 2 = 8 forms the right hand most part of the answer.

(ii) Now, diagonally multiply the first digit of the multiplicand (14) *i.e.*, 4 and second digit of the multiplier (12) *i.e.*, 1 (answer 4 × 1 = 4); then multiply the second digit of the multiplicand *i.e.*,1 and first digit of the multiplier i.e., 2 (answer 1 × 2 = 2); add these two *i.e.*,4 + 2 = 6. It gives the next, *i.e.*, second digit of the answer. Hence, second digit of the answer is 6.

(iii) Now, multiply the second digit of the multiplicand *i.e.*, 1 and second digit of the multiplier *i.e.*, 1 vertically, *i.e.*, 1 × 1 = 1. It gives the left hand most part of the answer.

Thus the answer is 16 8.

Symbolically we can represent the process as follows:

$$\begin{array}{cc} 1 & 4 \\ 1 & 2 \end{array}$$

The symbols are operated from right to left .

Step (i) :

$$1 \quad 4$$
$$1 \quad 2$$
$$: 4 \times 2$$

Step (ii) :

$$1 \quad 4$$
$$1 \quad 2$$
$$2 + 4 : 8$$

Step (iii) :

$$1 \quad 4$$
$$1 \quad 2$$
$$1 \times 1 : 6 : 8$$

which gives 168

(b) Multiplication of two 3 digit numbers

Ex: Find the product of 124×132.

Proceeding from right to left

(i) $4 \times 2 = 8$. First digit = 8

(ii) $(2 \times 2) + (3 \times 4) = 4 + 12 = 16$. The digit 6 is retained and 1 is carried over to left side. Second digit = 6.

(iii) $(1 \times 2) + (2 \times 3) + (1 \times 4) = 2 + 6 + 4 = 12$. The carried over 1 of above step is added *i.e.*, $12 + 1 = 13$. Now 3 is retained and 1 is carried over to left side. Thus third digit = 3.

(iv) $(1 \times 3) + (2 \times 1) = 3 + 2 = 5$. the carried over 1 of above step is added *i.e.*, $5 + 1 = 6$. It is retained. Thus fourth digit = 6

(v) $(1 \times 1) = 1$. As there is no carried over number from the previous step it is retained. Thus fifth digit = 1

$$124 \times 132 = 16368.$$

4. Paravartya Yojayet

'Paravartya – Yojayet' means 'transpose and apply'

(i) Consider the division by divisors of more than one digit, and when the divisors are slightly greater than powers of 10.

Example 1 : Divide 1225 by 12.

Step 1 : (From left to right) write the Divisor leaving the first digit, write the other digit or digits using negative (–) sign and place them below the divisor as shown.

$$12$$
$$\underline{-2}$$

Step 2 : Write down the dividend to the right. Set apart the last digit for the remainder.

i.e.,   12   122   5

        –2

Step 3 : Write the 1st digit below the horizontal line drawn under the dividend. Multiply the digit by –2, write the product below the 2nd digit and add.

i.e.,   12   122   5
        –2   –2
        ‾‾‾   ‾‾‾‾
                        10

Since 1 x –2 = –2 and 2 + (–2) = 0

Step 4 : We get second digits' sum as '0'. Multiply the second digits' sum thus obtained by –2 and writes the product under 3rd digit and add.

        12   122   5
        –2   –20
        ‾‾‾   ‾‾‾‾‾‾‾‾
                        102   5

Step 5 : Continue the process to the last digit.

i.e.,   12   122   5
        –2   –20   –4
        ‾‾‾   ‾‾‾‾‾‾‾‾
                        102   1

Step 6: The sum of the last digit is the Remainder and the result to its left is Quotient.

Thus Q = 102 and R = 1

5. Sunyam Samya Samuchyah

The Sutra says the 'Samuchyah is the same, that Samuchyah is Zero.' *i.e.*, it should be equated to zero. The term 'Samuccaya' has several meanings under different contexts.

(i) We interpret, 'Samuchyah' as a term which occurs as a common factor in all the terms concerned and proceed as follows.

Example 1: The equation $6x + 2x = 4x + 3x$ has the same factor 'x' in all its terms. Hence, by the sutra it is zero, *i.e.*, $x = 0$.

Otherwise we have to work like this:

$$6x + 2x = 4x + 3x$$
$$8x = 7x$$
$$8x - 7x = 0$$
$$x = 0$$

This is applicable not only for 'x' but also any such unknown quantity as follows.

Example 2: $5(x + 1) = 3(x + 1)$

No need to proceed in the usual procedure like

$$5x + 5 = 3x + 3$$
$$5x - 3x = 3 - 5$$
$$2x = -2 \text{ or } x = -2 \div 2 = -1$$

Simply think of the contextual meaning of 'Samuchyah'

Now Samuchyah is $(x + 1)$

$$x + 1 = 0 \quad \text{gives} \quad x = -1$$

(ii) Now we interpret 'Samuchyah' as product of independent terms in expressions like $(x + a)(x + b)$

Example 3: $(x + 3)(x + 4) = (x - 2)(x - 6)$

Here, Samuchyah is $3 \times 4 = 12 = -2 \times -6$

Since it is same, we derive $x = 0$

(iii) We interpret 'Samuchyah' as the sum of the denominators of two fractions having the same numerical numerator.

Example 4: $\dfrac{1}{3x - 2} + \dfrac{1}{2x - 1} = 0$

for this we proceed by taking L.C.M.

$$\frac{(2x-1)+(3x-2)}{(3x-2)(2x-1)} = 0$$

$$\frac{5x-3}{(3x-2)(2x-1)} = 0$$

$$5x - 3 = 0 \qquad 5x = 3 \qquad \Rightarrow \quad x = 3/5$$

Instead of this, we can directly put the Samuchyah *i.e.*, sum of the denominators

i.e., $3x - 2 + 2x - 1 = 5x - 3 = 0$

giving $5x = 3 \qquad x = 3/5$

It is true and applicable for all problems of the type

$$\frac{m}{ax+b}+\frac{m}{cx+d} = 0$$

Samuchyah is $ax + b + cx + d$ and solution is $(m \neq 0)$

$$x = \frac{-(b+d)}{(a+c)}$$

(iv) We now interpret 'Samuchyah' as combination or total.

If the sum of the numerators and the sum of the denominators be the same, then that sum = 0.

Example 5: $\qquad \dfrac{3x+4}{3x+5} = \dfrac{3x+5}{3x+4}$

Since $\qquad N_1 + N_2 = 3x + 4 + 3x + 5 = 6x + 9,$

And $\qquad D_1 + D_2 = 3x + 4 + 3x + 5 = 6x + 9$

We have $\qquad N_1 + N_2 = D_1 + D_2 = 6x + 9$

Hence, from Sunya Samuchyah we get $6x + 9 = 0$

$$6x = -9$$

$$x = \frac{-9}{6} = \frac{-3}{2}$$

6. Anurupye - Sunyamanyat

The Sutra says : 'If one is in ratio, the other one is zero'.

This Sutra is used in solving a special type of simultaneous simple equations in which the coefficients of 'one' variable are in the same ratio to each other as the independent terms are to each other. In such case the Sutra says the 'other' variable is zero from which we get two simple equations in the first variable (already considered) and of course give the same value for the variable.

Example 1:

$$3x + 7y = 2$$
$$4x + 21y = 6$$

Observe that the y-coefficients are in the ratio 7 : 21 *i.e.*, 1 : 3, which is same as the ratio of independent terms *i.e.*, 2 : 6 *i.e.*, 1 : 3. Hence the other variable $x = 0$ and $7y = 2$ or $21y = 6$ gives $y = 2/7$

Example 2:

$$323x + 147y = 1615$$
$$969x + 321y = 4845$$

The very appearance of the problem is frightening. But just an observation and anurupye sunyamanyat give the solution $x = 5$, because coefficient of x ratio is

323 : 969 = 1 : 3 and constant terms ratio is 1615 : 4845 = 1 : 3.

$y = 0$ and $323\,x = 1615$ or $969\,x = 4845$ gives $x = 5$.

In solving simultaneous quadratic equations, also we can take the help of the 'sutra' in the following way:

Example 3: Solve for x and y

$$x + 4y = 10$$
$$x^2 + 5xy + 4y^2 + 4x - 2y = 20$$

$x^2 + 5xy + 4y^2 + 4x - 2y = 20$ can be written as

$$(x + y)(x + 4y) + 4x - 2y = 20$$
$$10(x + y) + 4x - 2y = 20 \text{ (Since } x + 4y = 10)$$
$$10x + 10y + 4x - 2y = 20$$
$$14x + 8y = 20$$

Now $x + 4y = 10$

$$14x + 8y = 20 \text{ and } 4 : 8 :: 10 : 20$$

from the Sutra, $x = 0$ and $4y = 10$, *i.e.*, $8y = 20y = 10/4 = 2\frac{1}{2}$.

Thus **$x = 0$** and **$y = 2\frac{1}{2}$.** is the solution.

7. Sankalana - Vyavakalanabhyam

This Sutra means 'by addition and by subtraction'. It can be applied in solving a special type of simultaneous equations where the x-coefficients and the y-coefficients are found interchanged.

Example 1: $45x - 23y = 113$

$$23x - 45y = 91$$

In the conventional method we have to make equal either the coefficient of x or coefficient of y in both the equations. For that we have to multiply equation (1) by 45 and equation (2) by 23 and subtract to get the value of x and then substitute the value of x in one of the equations to get the value of y or we have to multiply equation (1) by 23 and equation (2) by 45 and then subtract to get value of y and then substitute the value of y in one of the equations, to get the value of x. It is difficult process to think of.

From Sankalana – vyavakalanabhyam

add them,

   i.e., $(45x - 23y) + (23x - 45y) = 113 + 91$

   i.e., $68x - 68y = 204$ $\therefore x - y = 3$

subtract one from other,

   i.e., $(45x - 23y) - (23x - 45y) = 113 - 91$

   i.e., $22x + 22y = 22$ $\therefore x + y = 1$

and repeat the same sutra, we get $x = 2$ and $y = -1$

Example 2:

$$1955x - 476y = 2482$$

$$476x - 1955y = -4913$$

just add, $2431 (x - y) = -2431$ $\therefore x - y = -1$

subtract, $1479 (x + y) = 7395$ $\therefore x + y = 5$

once again add, $2x = 4$ $\therefore x = 2$

subtract, $-2y = -6$ $\therefore y = 3$

8. Puranapuranabhyam

The Sutra can be taken as Purana - Apuranabhyam which means by the completion or non - completion. Its application is used in solving the roots for general form of quadratic equation.

We have : $ax^2 + bx + c = 0$

$$x^2 + (b/a)x + c/a = 0 \text{ (dividing by a)}$$

$$x^2 + (b/a)x = -c/a$$

completing the square (*i.e.*, purana) on the L.H.S.

$$x^2 + (b/a)x + (b^2/4a^2) = -c/a + (b^2/4a^2)$$

$$[x + (b/2a)]^2 = (b^2 - 4ac)/4a^2$$

Proceeding in this way we finally get $x = \dfrac{-b \pm \sqrt{b^2 - 4ac}}{2a}$

Now we apply purana to solve problems given below:

Example 1. $x^3 + 6x^2 + 11x + 6 = 0.$

Since $(x + 2)^3 = x^3 + 6x^2 + 12x + 8$

Add $(x + 2)$ to both sides

We get $x^3 + 6x^2 + 11x + 6 + x + 2 = x + 2$

i.e., $x^3 + 6x^2 + 12x + 8 = x + 2$

i.e., $(x + 2)^3 = (x + 2)$

this is of the form $y^3 = y$ for $y = x + 2$

solution $y = 0, y = 1, y = -1$

i.e., $x + 2 = 0, 1, -1$

which gives $x = -2, -1, -3$

Example 2: $x^3 + 8x^2 + 17x + 10 = 0$

We know $(x + 3)^3 = x^3 + 9x^2 + 27x + 27$

So adding on the both sides, the term $(x^2 + 10x + 17)$, we get

$$x^3 + 8x^2 + 17x + x^2 + 10x + 17 = x^2 + 10x + 17$$

i.e., $x^3 + 9x^2 + 27x + 27 = x^2 + 6x + 9 + 4x + 8$

i.e., $(x + 3)^3 = (x + 3)^2 + 4(x + 3) - 4$

$$y^3 = y^2 + 4y - 4 \text{ for } y = x + 3$$

$$y = 1, 2, -2.$$

Hence $$x = -2, -1, -5$$

Further purana can be applied in solving Biquadratic equations also.

9. Calana - Kalanabhyam

The Sutra means 'Sequential motion'.

(i) In the first instance it is used to find the roots of a quadratic equation $7x^2 - 11x - 7 = 0$. The sutra is also called as calculus formula. Its application at that point is as follows. Now by calculus formula we say: $14x - 11 = \pm\sqrt{317}$.

(ii) At the Second instance for factorizing expressions of 3rd, 4th and 5th degree, the procedure is mentioned as 'Vedic Sutras relating to Calana – Kalana – Differential Calculus'.

10. Ekanyunena Purvena

This Sutra comes as a Sub-sutra to Nikhilam which gives the meaning 'One less than the previous' or 'One less than the one before'.

1. The use of this sutra in case of multiplication by 9,99,999... is as follows

Method :

(a) The left hand side digit (digits) is (are) obtained by applying the ekanyunena purvena *i.e.,* by deduction 1 from the left side digit (digits).

   e.g. (i) 6×9; $6 - 1 = 5$ (L.H.S. digit)

(b) The right hand side digit is the complement or difference between the multiplier and the left hand side digit (digits). *i.e.,* 6×9 R.H.S is $9 - 5 = 4$.

(c) The two numbers give the answer; *i.e.* $6 \times 9 = 54$.

   Example 1: 8×9

   Step (a) gives $8 - 1 = 7$ (L.H.S. Digit)

   Step (b) gives $9 - 7 = 2$ (R.H.S. Digit)

   Step (c) gives the answer 72.

Example 2: 25 × 99

Step (a) : 25 − 1 = 24

Step (b) : 99 − 24 = 75 (or 100 − 25)

Step (c) : 25 × 99 = 2475.

Example 3: 34 × 99

Answer :
$$\frac{\begin{array}{c}(34-1)\\=33\end{array} \Big/ \begin{array}{c}(99-33)\\=66\,(\text{or}\,100-34)\end{array}}{} = 3366$$

Example 4: 346 × 999

Answer :
$$\frac{\begin{array}{c}(346-1)\\=345\end{array} \Big/ \begin{array}{c}(999-345)\\=654\end{array}}{} = 345654$$

Example 5: 878 × 9999

Answer :
$$\frac{\begin{array}{c}(878-1)\\=877\end{array} \Big/ \begin{array}{c}(9999-877)\\=9122\,(10000-878)\end{array}}{} = 8779122$$

Note the process : The multiplicand has to be reduced by 1 to obtain the LHS and the rightside is mechanically obtained by the subtraction of the L.H.S from the multiplier which is practically a direct application of Nikhilam Sutra.

Note: Now the remaining sutras:

10. Yavadunam (The deficiency)

11. Vyastisamastih (Whole as one and one as whole)

12. Sesanyan Kena Caramena (Remainder by the last digit)

13. Sopantyadvayamantyam (Ultimate and twice the penultimate)

15. Gunitasamuchyah (The whole product is the same)

16. Gunaka Samuchyah (Collectivity of multipliers)

These Sutras have their applications in solving different problems in different contexts. Further they are used along with other Sutras. So they are not dealt here seperately.

SUB - SUTRAS

Some important sub-sutras with examples are given below:

I. Anurupyena

The upa-Sutra 'anurupyena' means 'proportionality'. This Sutra is highly useful to find products of two numbers when both of them are near the Common bases *i.e.,* powers of base 10 . It is very clear that in such cases the expected 'Simplicity ' in doing problems is absent.

Example 1: 46 × 43

As per the previous methods, if we select 100 as base we get

$$46 -54 \quad \text{This is much more difficult and of no use.}$$
$$43 -57$$

Now by 'anurupyena' we consider a working base In three ways. We can solve the problem.

Method 1: Take the nearest higher multiple of 10. In this case it is 50.

Treat it as 100/2 = 50. Now the steps are as follows:

(i) Choose the working base near to the numbers under consideration.

i.e., working base is 100/2 = 50

(ii) Write the numbers one below the other

i.e.
$$4 \quad 6$$
$$4 \quad 3$$

(iii) Write the differences of the two numbers respectively from 50 against each number on right side

i.e.
$$46 \quad -04$$
$$43 \quad -07$$

(iv) Write cross-subtraction or cross- addition as the case may be under the line drawn.

$$46 \qquad -04$$
$$43 \qquad -07$$
$$\overline{(46-7) \text{ or}}$$
$$(43-4)$$
$$= 39$$

(v) Multiply the differences and write the product in the left side of the answer.

$$\begin{array}{cc} 46 & -04 \\ 43 & -07 \\ \hline 39 / -4 \times -7 & = 28 \end{array}$$

(vi) Since base is $100 / 2 = 50$, 39 in the answer represents 39×50.

Hence divide 39 by 2 because $50 = 100/2$

Thus $39 \div 2$ gives $19\frac{1}{2}$ where 19 is quotient and 1 is remainder. This 1 as Reminder gives one 50 making the L.H.S of the answer $28 + 50 = 78$ (or Remainder $\frac{1}{2} \times 100 + 28$)

i.e. R.H.S 19 and L.H.S 78 together give the answer 1978. We represent it as

$$\begin{array}{rcc} & 46 & -04 \\ & 43 & -07 \\ \hline 2) & 39 & / \quad 28 \\ \hline & 19\frac{1}{2} & / \quad 28 \\ & = 19 & / \ 78 = 1978 \end{array}$$

Example 2: 42×48.

With $100/2 = 50$ as working base, the problem is as follows:

$$\begin{array}{rcc} & 42 & -08 \\ & 48 & -02 \\ \hline 2) & 40 & / \quad 16 \\ \hline & 20 & / \quad 16 \\ & 42 \times 48 & = 2016 \end{array}$$

Method 2: For the example 1: 46×43. We take the same working base 50. We treat it as $50 = 5 \times 10$. *i.e.* we operate with 10 but not with 100 as in method now

$$
\begin{array}{ll}
46 & -04 \\
43 & -07 \\
\hline
(46-7)\,\text{or} & -4\times -7 \\
(43-4)=39 & = {}_28 \\
\hline
39\times 5+2 & 8 \\
(\text{carried over}) &
\end{array}
$$

$$(195 + 2)\,/\,8 = 1978$$

[Since we operate with 10, the R.H.S portion shall have only unit place. Hence out of the product 28, 2 is carried over to left side. The L.H.S portion of the answer shall be multiplied by 5, since we have taken $50 = 5 \times 10$.]

Now in the example 2: 42 x 48 we can carry as follows by treating $50 = 5 \times 10$

$$
\begin{array}{ll}
42 & -08 \\
48 & -02 \\
\hline
40 & {}_16 \\
\times 5 & \\
\hline
200 & {}_16 \quad = 2016
\end{array}
$$

Method 3: We take the nearest lower multiple of 10 since the numbers are 46 and 43 as in the first example, We consider 40 as working base and treat it as 4×10.

$$
\begin{array}{ll}
46 & 06 \\
43 & 03 \\
\hline
(46+3)\,\text{or} & 6\times 3 \\
(43+6)=49 & = {}_18
\end{array}
$$

Since 10 is in operation 1 is carried out digit in 18.

Since 4×10 is working base we consider 49×4 on L.H.S of answer *i.e.* 196 and 1 carried over the left side, giving L.H.S. of answer as 1978. Hence the answer is 1978.

We proceed in the same method for 42 × 48

```
42     02
48     08        working base 4 × 10 = 40
─────────
50  /  ₁6
× 4 /            since 10 is in operation
─────────
200 / ₁6         = 2016
```

2. Adyamadyenantya - Mantyena

The Sutra 'adyamadyenantya-mantyena' means 'the first by the first and the last by the last'.

Suppose we are asked to find out the area of a rectangular card board whose length and breadth are respectively 6ft. 4 inches and 5 ft. 8 inches. Generally we continue the problem like this.

$$\text{Area} = \text{Length} \times \text{Breath}$$
$$= 6'4'' \times 5'\ 8'' \quad \text{Since } 1' = 12'', \text{ conversion}$$
$$= (6 \times 12 + 4)(5 \times 12 + 8) \text{ in to single unit}$$
$$= 76''\ 68'' = 5168 \text{ Sq. inches.}$$

Since 1 sq. ft. = 12 × 12 = 144 sq. inches we have area

```
5168
──── = 144) 5168 (35
144          432
           ─────
            848
            720        i.e., 35 Sq. ft 128 Sq. inches
           ─────
            128
```

But by Vedic principles we proceed in the way "the first by first and the last by last"

i.e., 6' 4'' can be treated as $6x + 4$ and 5' 8'' as $5x + 8$,

Where x = 1ft. = 12 in; x^2 is sq. ft.

Now $(6x + 4)(5x + 8)$

$$= 30x^2 + 6.8.x + 4.5.x + 32$$
$$= 30x^2 + 48x + 20x + 32$$
$$= 30x^2 + 68.x + 32$$

$$= 30x^2 + (5x + 8).\, x + 32 \text{ (Writing } 68 = 5 \times 12 + 8)$$
$$= 35x^2 + 8.\, x + 32$$
$$= 35 \text{ Sq. ft.} + 8 \times 12 \text{ Sq. inches} + 32 \text{ Sq. inches}$$
$$= 35 \text{ Sq. ft.} + 96 \text{ Sq. inches} + 32 \text{ Sq. inches}$$
$$= 35 \text{ Sq. ft.} + 128 \text{ Sq. inches}$$

It is interesting to know that a mathematically untrained and even uneducated carpenter simply works in this way by mental argumentation. It goes in his mind like this

$$6'\quad 4''$$
$$5'\quad 8''$$

First by first *i.e.*, $6' \times 5' = 30$ sq. ft.

Last by last *i.e.* $4'' \times 8'' = 32$ sq. in.

Now cross wise $6 \times 8 + 5 \times 4 = 48 + 20 = 68$.

Adjust as many '12' s as possible towards left as 'units' *i.e.*, 68 $= 5 \times 12 + 8$, 5 twelve's as 5 square feet make the first $30 + 5 = 35$ sq. ft; 8 left becomes 8×12 square inches and go towards right *i.e.*, $8 \times 12 = 96$ sq. in. towards right ives $96 + 32 = 128$ sq.in.

Thus he got area in some sort of 35 sq. uints and another sort of 128 sq. units. *i.e.*, 35 sq. ft 128 sq. in.

3. Yavadunam Tavadunikrtya Varganca Yojayet

The meaning of the Sutra is 'what ever the deficiency subtract that deficit from the number and write along side the square of that deficit'.

This Sutra can be applicable to obtain squares of numbers close to bases of powers of 10.

Method-1 : Numbers near and less than the bases of powers of 10.

Eg 1: 9^2 Here base is 10.

The answer is separated into two parts by a'/'

Note that deficit is $10 - 9 = 1$

Multiply the deficit by itself or square it

$1^2 = 1$. As the deficiency is 1, subtract it from the number *i.e.*, $9 - 1 = 8$.

Now put 8 on the left and 1 on the right side of the vertical line or slash *i.e.*, 8/1.

Hence 81 is answer.

Eg. 2: 95^2 Here base is 100.

Since deficit is $100 - 95 = 5$ and square of it is 25 and the deficiency subtracted from the number 95 gives $95 - 5 = 90$, we get the answer 90/25

Thus $95^2 = 9025$.

Eg. 3: 994^2 Base is 1000

Deficit is $1000 - 994 = 6$. Square of it is 36.

Deficiency subtracted from 994 gives $994 - 6 = 988$

Answer is 988 / 036 [since base is 1000]

Eg. 4: 9988^2 Base is 10,000.

Deficit $= 10000 - 9988 = 12$.

Square of deficit $= 12^2 = 144$.

Deficiency subtracted from number $= 9988 - 12 = 9976$.

Answer is 9976 / 0144 [since base is 10,000] $= 99760144$

Eg. 5: 88^2 Base is 100.

Deficit $= 100 - 88 = 12$.

Square of deficit $= 12^2 = 144$.

Deficiency subtracted from number $= 88 - 12 = 76$.

Now answer is 76/$_1$44 $=7744$ [since base is 100]

Method. 2 : Numbers near and greater than the bases of powers of 10.

Eg.(1): 13^2.

Instead of subtracting the deficiency from the number we add and proceed as in Method-1.

for 13^2, base is 10, surplus is 3.

Surplus added to the number $= 13 + 3 = 16$.

Square of surplus $= 3^2 = 9$

Answer is 16/9 $= 169$.

Eg.(2): 114^2

Base = 100, Surplus = 14,

Square of surplus = 14^2 = 196

add surplus to number = 114 + 14 = 128.

Answer is 128/$_1$96 = 12996.

Method 3: This is applicable to numbers which are near to multiples of 10, 100, 1000 .... etc. For this we combine two upa-Sutra 'anurupyena' and 'yavadunam tavadunikritya varganca yojayet' together.

Example 1: 388^2 Nearest base = 400.

We treat 400 as 4 × 100. As the number is less than the base we proceed as follows

Number 388, deficit = 400 − 388 = 12

Since it is less than base, deduct the deficit

i.e., 388 − 12 = 376.

multiply this result by 4 since base is 4 × 100 = 400.

376 × 4 = 1504

Square of deficit = 12^2 = 144.

Hence answer is 1504/$_1$44 = 150544 [since we have taken multiples of 100].

Example 2: 475^2 Nearest base = 500.

Treat 500 as 5 × 100 and proceed

475^2 = (475 − 25)/25^2 [since deficit is 25]

$$= 450 \;/_6\, 25 \times 5$$

since 500 base is taken as 5 × 100 and 6 of 625 is carried over

$$= 2250/_6 25$$

$$= 225625$$

Cubing of Numbers:

With a slight modification yavadunam can also be applied for finding the cubes of numbers.

Example : Find the cube of the number 106.

We proceed as follows:

(i) For 106, Base is 100. The surplus is 6.

Here we add double of the surplus *i.e.* 106 + 12 = 118.

(Like in squaring, we directly add the surplus)

This makes the left-hand-most part of the answer.

i.e. answer proceeds like 118 / - - - - -

(ii) Put down the new surplus *i.e.* 118 − 100 = 18 multiplied by the initial surplus *i.e.* 6 = 108.

Since base is 100, we write 108 in carried over form 108 *i.e.* .

As this is middle portion of the answer, the answer proceeds like 118/$_1$08 /....

(iii) Write down the cube of initial surplus *i.e.* 6^3 = 216 as the last portion *i.e.*, right hand side last portion of the answer.

Since base is 100, write 216 as $_2$16 as 2 is to be carried over.

Answer is 118/$_1$08/$_2$16

Now proceeding from right to left and adjusting the carried over, we get the answer

119/10/16 = 1191016.

Eg.(1): 103^3 = (103 + 6)/9 × 3/3^3

= 109/27/27

= 1092727.

Observe initial surplus = 3, next surplus = 9 and base = 100.

4. Antyayor Dasakepi

The Sutra signifies numbers of which the last digits added up give 10. *i.e.,* the Sutra works in multiplication of numbers for example: 25 and 25, 47 and 43, 62 and 68, 116 and 114. Note that in each case the sum of the last digit of first number to the last digit of second number is 10. Further the portion of digits or numbers left wards to the last digits remain the same. At that instant use Ekadhikena on left hand side digits. Multiplication of the last digits gives the right hand part of the answer.

Example 1 : 47 × 43

Observe the end digits sum 7 + 3 = 10; then by the sutras antyayor dasakepi and ekadhikena we have the answer.

$$47 \times 43 = (4 + 1) \times 4 / 7 \times 3$$
$$= 20 / 21$$
$$= 2021.$$

Example 2: 62 × 68

2 + 8 = 10, L.H.S. portion remains the same *i.e.*, 6.

Ekadhikena of 6 gives 7

$$62 \times 68 = (6 \times 7)/(2 \times 8)$$
$$= 42 / 16$$
$$= 4216.$$

Example 3: 127 × 123

As antyayor dasakepi works, we apply ekadhikena

$$127 \times 123 = 12 \times 13 / 7 \times 3$$
$$= 156 / 21$$
$$= 15621.$$

5. Antyayoreva

This means 'only the last terms'. This is useful in solving simple equations of those whose numerator and denominator on the L.H.S. bearing the independent terms stand in the same ratio to each other as the entire numerator and the entire denominator of the R.H.S. stand to each other.

Example 1:

$$\frac{x^2 + 2x + 7}{x^2 + 3x + 5} = \frac{x + 2}{x + 3}$$

In the conventional method we proceed as

$$\frac{x^2 + 2x + 7}{x^2 + 3x + 5} = \frac{x + 2}{x + 3}$$

$$(x + 3)(x^2 + 2x + 7) = (x + 2)(x^2 + 3x + 5)$$

$$x^3 + 2x^2 + 7x + 3x^2 + 6x + 21 = x^3 + 3x^2 + 5x + 2x^2 + 6x + 10$$

$$x^3 + 5x^2 + 13x + 21 = x^3 + 5x^2 + 11x + 10$$

Canceling like terms on both sides

$$13x + 21 = 11x + 10$$
$$13x - 11x = 10 - 21$$
$$2x = -11$$
$$x = -11/2$$

Now we solve the problem using antyayoreva.

$$\frac{x^2 + 2x + 7}{x^2 + 3x + 5} = \frac{x + 2}{x + 3}$$

Consider

$$\frac{x^2 + 2x + 7}{x^2 + 3x + 5} = \frac{x + 2}{x + 3}$$

Observe that

$$\frac{x^2 + 2x}{x^2 + 3x} = \frac{x(x + 2)}{x(x + 3)} = \frac{x + 2}{x + 3}$$

This is according to the condition in the sutra. Hence from the sutra

$$\frac{x + 2}{x + 3} = \frac{7}{5}$$
$$5x + 10 = 7x + 21$$
$$7x - 5x = -21 + 10$$
$$2x = -11$$
$$x = -11 / 2$$

6. Lopana Sthapanabhyam

Lopana sthapanabhyam means 'by alternate elimination and retention'.

Consider the case of factorization of quadratic equation of type $ax^2 + by^2 + cz^2 + dxy + eyz + fzx$. This is a homogeneous equation of second degree in three variables x, y, z. The sub-sutra removes the difficulty and makes the factorization simple. The steps are as follows:

(i) Eliminate z by putting $z = 0$ and retain x and y and factorize thus obtained a quadratic in x and y by means of 'adyamadyena' sutra.

(ii) Similarly eliminate y and retain x and z and factorize the quadratic in x and z.

(iii) With these two sets of factors, fill in the gaps caused by the elimination process of z and y respectively. This gives actual factors of the expression.

Example 1: $3x^2 + 7xy + 2y^2 + 11xz + 7yz + 6z^2$.

Step (i): Eliminate z and retain x, y; factorize
$$3x^2 + 7xy + 2y^2 = (3x + y)(x + 2y)$$

Step (ii): Eliminate y and retain x, z; factorize
$$3x^2 + 11xz + 6z^2 = (3x + 2z)(x + 3z)$$

Step (iii): Fill the gaps, the given expression
$$= (3x + y + 2z)(x + 2y + 3z)$$

Example 2: $12x^2 + 11xy + 2y^2 - 13xz - 7yz + 3z^2$.

Step (i): Eliminate z *i.e.*, $z = 0$; factorize
$$12x^2 + 11xy + 2y^2 = (3x + 2y)(4x + y)$$

Step (ii): Eliminate y *i.e.*, $y = 0$; factorize
$$12x^2 - 13xz + 3z^2 = (4x - 3z)(3x - z)$$

Step (iii): Fill in the gaps; the given expression
$$= (4x + y - 3z)(3x + 2y - z)$$

Example 3: $3x^2 + 6y^2 + 2z^2 + 11xy + 7yz + 6xz + 19x + 22y + 13z + 20$

Step (i): Eliminate y and z, retain x and independent term
i.e., $y = 0$, $z = 0$ in the expression (E).
Then $E = 3x^2 + 19x + 20 = (x + 5)(3x + 4)$

Step (ii): Eliminate z and x, retain y and independent term
i.e., $z = 0$, $x = 0$ in the expression.
Then $E = 6y^2 + 22y + 20 = (2y + 4)(3y + 5)$

Step (iii): Eliminate x and y, retain z and independent term
i.e., $x = 0$, $y = 0$ in the expression.
Then $E = 2z^2 + 13z + 20 = (z + 4)(2z + 5)$

Step (iv): The expression has the factors (think of independent terms)
$$= (3x + 2y + z + 4)(x + 3y + 2z + 5).$$

In this way either homogeneous equations of second degree or general equations of second degree in three variables can be very easily solved by applying 'adyamadyena' and 'lopanasthapanabhyam' sutras.

7. Vilokanam

The Sutra 'Vilokanam' means 'Observation'. Generally we come across problems which can be solved by mere observation. But we follow the same conventional procedure and obtain the solution. But the Sutra enables us to observe the problem completely and find the pattern and finally solve the problem by just observation.

Let us take the equation $x + (1/x) = 5/2$. The conventional process tends us to solve the problem in the following way.

$$x + \frac{1}{x} = \frac{5}{2}$$

$$\frac{x^2 + 1}{x} = \frac{5}{2}$$

$$2x^2 + 2 = 5x$$

$$2x^2 - 5x + 2 = 0$$

$$2x^2 - 4x - x + 2 = 0$$

$$2x\,(x - 2) - (x - 2) = 0$$

$$(x - 2)\,(2x - 1) = 0$$

$$x - 2 = 0 \text{ gives } x = 2$$

$$2x - 1 = 0 \text{ gives } x = \tfrac{1}{2}$$

But by Vilokanam *i.e.*, observation

$$x + \frac{1}{x} = \frac{5}{2} \text{ can be viewed as}$$

$$x + \frac{1}{x} = 2 + \frac{1}{2} \text{ giving } x = 2 \text{ or } \tfrac{1}{2}.$$

Example 1 :

$$\frac{x}{x+2} + \frac{x+2}{x} = \frac{34}{15}$$

In the conventional process, we have to take L.C.M, cross-multiplication. simplification and factorization. But Vilokanam gives

$$\frac{34}{15} = \frac{9+25}{5\times 3} = \frac{3}{5} + \frac{5}{3}$$

$$\frac{x}{x+2} + \frac{x+2}{x} = \frac{3}{5} + \frac{5}{3}$$

gives $\qquad \dfrac{x}{x+2} = \dfrac{3}{5}$ or $\dfrac{5}{3}$

$$5x = 3x + 6 \quad \text{or} \quad 3x = 5x + 10$$

$$2x = 6 \quad \text{or} \quad -2x = 10$$

$$x = 3 \quad \text{or} \quad x = -5$$

Example 2 :

$$\frac{x+5}{x+6} + \frac{x+6}{x+5} = \frac{113}{56}$$

Now, $\qquad \dfrac{113}{56} = \dfrac{49+64}{7\times 8} = \dfrac{7}{8} + \dfrac{8}{7}$

$$\frac{x+5}{x+6} = \frac{7}{8} \quad \text{or} \quad \frac{x+5}{x+6} = \frac{8}{7}$$

$$8x + 40 = 7x + 42 \quad \text{or} \quad 7x + 35 = 8x + 48$$

$$x = 42 - 40 = 2 \quad \text{or} \quad -x = 48 - 35 = 13$$

$$x = 2 \quad \text{or} \quad x = -13.$$

8. Gunita Samuchyah : Samuchya Gunitah

This sub-sutra is intended for the purpose of verifying the correctness of obtained answers in multiplications, divisions and factorizations. It means in this context:

'The product of the sum of the coefficients **sc** in the factors is equal to the sum of the coefficients **sc** in the product'

Symbolically we represent as **sc** of the product = product of the **sc** (in the factors)

Example 1: $(x + 4)(x + 3) = x^2 + 7x + 12$

Now $(x + 4)(x + 3) = 5 \times 4 = 20$: Thus verified.

Example 2: $(x - 4)(2x + 5) = 2x^2 - 3x - 20$

Sc of the product $2 - 3 - 20 = -21$

Product of the **Sc** $= (1 - 4)(2 + 5) = (-3)(7) = -21$. Hence verified.

In case of cubics, biquadratics also the same rule applies.

We have $(x + 2)(x + 3)(x + 4) = x^3 + 9x^2 + 26x + 24$

Sc of the product $= 1 + 9 + 26 + 24 = 60$

Product of the **Sc** $= (1 + 2)(1 + 3)(1 + 4)$

$$= 3 \times 4 \times 5 = 60. \text{ Verified.}$$

Example 3: $(x + 5)(x + 7)(x - 2) = x^3 + 10x^2 + 11x - 70$

$(1 + 5)(1 + 7)(1 - 2) = 1 + 10 + 11 - 70$

i.e.,　　　　$6 \times 8 \times -1 = 22 - 70$

i.e.,　　　　$-48 = -48$ Verified.

We apply and interpret **So** and **Sc** as sum of the coefficients of the odd powers and sum of the coefficients of the even powers and derive that **So** = **Sc** gives $(x + 1)$ is a factor for the concerned expression in the variable x. **Sc** = 0 gives $(x - 1)$ is a factor.

EFFORTLESS MULTIPLICATIONS

Once a person decided to fulfill his desire. Only he didn't have enough strength to do it. Then he turned to his mother:

— *Mother, help me!*

— *Darling, I would be glad to help you, only I don't have the solution to your problem. And everything I have, I have already given to you…*

He asked a wise man:

— *Master, tell me from where can I get strength?*

— *The master replied, "It is said that it is on the Everest. But I couldn't find anything there, except the snowy winds".*

He asked the hermit:

— *Holy Father, where to find strength for realizing my dream?*

— *In your prayers, my son. And if your dream is false, you will understand it and find peace in your prayers…*

Who didn't the person ask, but the result of his search was only confusion.

— *Why are you so confused?,—asked an old man passing by.*

— *I have a dream, good man. But I don't know where to find strength for realizing it. I have asked everyone already—from Everest to hell. But there was no one who could help me.*

— *Not everyone,—a light flashed in an old man's eyes,—did you ask yourself?*

Multiplication is one of the most basic processes of Mathematics. Lots of problems are based on multiplication. In conventional way of mathematics, multiplication is considered as the backbone of Square, Cube etc. The conventional way of multiplication is taught in schools and is applicable to all types of numbers. There is no second method for finding the answer of multiplication and it becomes tedious as the number of digits increases. This might be the reason that even some college level students find it difficult when they are asked to solve 5 × 5 digit multiplication. One more disadvantage of following conventional way is that you cannot tell the answer mentally without using pen and paper.

While on the other hand, if you compare the Vedic way of doing multiplication, it is similar to conventional way, but definitely it is more efficient. After some practice, anyone can solve the questions orally in no time.

There are various methods of multiplication which are given below:

- **Multiplication by the Base Method.**

- **Multiplication by the Crosswise Method.**

MULTIPLICATION BY THE BASE METHOD

Base numbers are formed with the help of 0 and 1 such as 10, 100, 1000 and so on.

Base number is the first number to come in all digits. For example, 10 comes first in 2 digit numbers, 100 comes first in 3 digit numbers and so on.

When we talk about multiplication by the base method, 3 different cases are possible, which are

- When both the numbers are above the base number.

- When both the numbers are below the base number.

- When one number is above and another number is below the base.

> **Note:** *Please use this method when both the numbers are near to base numbers.*

Americans called Mathematics "Math", arguing that "Mathematics" functions as a singular noun so "Math" should be singular to.

When both the Numbers are above the Base Number

Let us first talk about the numbers which are near to base 10.

Example 4.1: Solve 12 × 15.

Solution:

Step 1.   Here the nearest base is 10

Step 2.   Write down both the numbers one above the other and their differences with respect to the base on the right hand side with their respective signs as shown below

$$12 + 02 \ (+2 = 12 - 10 \ )$$

$$15 + 05 \ (+5 = 15 - 10 \ )$$

Step 3:   Draw a vertical line to divide the given space into 2 boxes *i.e.*, LHB and RHB as shown below

$$
\begin{array}{c|c}
12 & +2 \\
15 & +5 \\
\hline
\text{LHB} & \text{RHB}
\end{array}
$$

Step 4:   The value of RHB can be calculated by multiplying the two numbers which are placed above the RHB as shown below

$$
\begin{array}{c|c}
12 & +2 \\
15 & +5 \\
\hline
\text{LHB} & +10
\end{array} \times
$$

** Write the Digits in RHB with Sign (*i.e.*, + or –)

Step 5:   The value of LHB can be calculated by adding any two numbers with sign diagonally as shown below

$$
\begin{array}{c|c}
12 & +2 \\
15 & +5 \\
\hline
17 & +10
\end{array}
\quad \text{or} \quad
\begin{array}{c|c}
12 & +2 \\
15 & +5 \\
\hline
17 & +10
\end{array}
$$

> **Note:** *In this method RHB will contain only one digit, rest all the digits will be added with the digits present in LHB by following carryover system.*

$$
\begin{array}{c|c}
12 & +2 \\
15 & +5 \\
\hline
17 & +10
\end{array}
$$

$$
\begin{array}{c|c}
12 & +2 \\
15 & +5 \\
\hline
18 & 0
\end{array}
$$

$$12 \times 15 = 180$$

Example 4.2: 13 × 17.

Solution:

Step 1:   Here the nearest base is 10

Step 2:

$$\begin{array}{c|c} 13 & +3 \\ 17 & +7 \\ \hline \text{LHB} & \text{RHB} \end{array}$$

Step 3:

$$\begin{array}{c|c} 13 & +3 \\ 17 & +7 \end{array} \Big\} \times$$

$$\begin{array}{c|c} \hline \text{LHB} & +21 \end{array}$$

Step 4:

$$\begin{array}{c|c} 13 & +3 \\ 17 & +7 \\ \hline 20 & +21 \end{array}$$

$$20 \mid 21$$

$$= 221 \text{ Ans.}$$

Let us now talk about the numbers which are near to base 100.

Example 4.3: 103 × 109

Solution:

Step 1:   Here the nearest base is 100

Step 2:

$$\begin{array}{c|c} 103 & +3 \\ 109 & +9 \\ \hline \text{LHB} & \text{RHB} \end{array}$$

Step 3:

$$\begin{array}{c|c} 103 & +3 \\ 109 & +9 \end{array} \Big\} \times$$

$$\begin{array}{c|c} \hline \text{LHB} & +27 \end{array}$$

Step 4:

$$\begin{array}{c|c} 103 & +3 \\ 109 & +9 \\ \hline 112 & +27 \end{array}$$

$$112 \mid +27$$

$$= 11227 \text{ Ans.}$$

> **Note:** *RHB will always contains same number of digits as to number of zero in the nearest base of the given number.*

Example 4.4: 113 × 112.

Solution:

Step 1:   Nearest base is 100

Step 2:
$$
\begin{array}{c|c}
113 & +13 \\
112 & +12 \\
\hline
\text{LHB} & \text{RHB}
\end{array}
$$

Step 3:
$$
\left.\begin{array}{c|c}
113 & +13 \\
112 & +12
\end{array}\right\} \times
$$
$$
\begin{array}{c|c}
\text{LHB} & +156
\end{array}
$$

Step 4:
$$
\begin{array}{c|c}
113 & +13 \\
112 & +12 \\
\hline
125 & +156 \\
125 & +156
\end{array}
$$

$$= 12656 \textbf{ Ans.}$$

Let us now talk about the numbers which are near to base 1000.

Example 4.5: 1003 × 1021.

Solution:

Step 1:   Nearest base is 1000

Step 2:
$$
\begin{array}{c|c}
1003 & +003 \\
1021 & +021 \\
\hline
\text{LHB} & \text{RHB}
\end{array}
$$

Step 3:
$$
\left.\begin{array}{c|c}
1003 & +003 \\
1021 & +021
\end{array}\right\} \times
$$
$$
\begin{array}{c|c}
\text{LHB} & +063
\end{array}
$$

Step 4:

$$
\begin{array}{c|l}
1003 \; \diagdown \; +003 & \\
1021 \quad\; +021 & \\
\hline
1024 \;\mid\; +063 \\
1024 \;\mid\; +063 \\
\end{array}
$$

$$= 1024063 \textbf{ Ans.}$$

Teacher: Today, we're going to talk about the tenses. Now, if I say "I am beautiful," which tense is it?

Student: Obviously it is past tense.

Example 4.6: 1114 × 1008.

Solution:

Step 1: Nearest base is 1000

Step 2:

$$
\begin{array}{c|l}
1114 & +114 \\
1008 & +008 \\
\hline
\text{LHB} & \text{RHB} \\
\end{array}
$$

Step 3:

$$
\left.
\begin{array}{c l}
1114 & +114 \\
1008 & +008 \\
\end{array}
\right\} \times
$$

$$
\begin{array}{c|l}
\hline
\text{LHB} & +912 \\
\end{array}
$$

Step 4:

$$
\begin{array}{c|l}
1114 \; \diagdown \; +114 & \\
1008 \quad\; +008 & \\
\hline
1122 \;\mid\; +912 \\
1122 \;\mid\; +912 \\
\end{array}
$$

$$= 1122912 \textbf{ Ans.}$$

Exercise for Practice

Solve the following questions:

1.	111 × 113	**2.**	108 × 114
3.	106 × 116	**4.**	101 × 117
5.	103 × 109	**6.**	1012 × 1009
7.	1005 × 1011	**8.**	1003 × 1016
9.	1008 × 1001	**10.**	1017 × 1006

When both the Numbers are below the Base Number

Let us first talk about the numbers which are near to base 10.

Example 4.7: Solve 7 × 9.

Solution:

Step 1: Here the nearest base is 10

Step 2: Write down both the numbers one above the other and their differences with respect to the base on the right hand side with their respective signs as shown below

$$7 - 3 \ (-3 = 7 - 10)$$
$$9 - 1 \ (-1 = 9 - 10)$$

Step 3: Draw a vertical line to divide the given space into 2 boxes, *i.e.*, LHB and RHB as shown below

$$
\begin{array}{c|c}
7 & -3 \\
9 & -1 \\
\hline
\text{LHB} & \text{RHB}
\end{array}
$$

Step 4: The value of RHB can be calculated by multiplying the two numbers which are placed above the RHB as shown below

$$
\begin{array}{c|c}
7 & -3 \\
9 & -1 \\
\hline
\text{LHB} & +3
\end{array}
$$

Step 5: The value of LHB can be calculated by adding any two numbers with sign diagonally as shown below

$$
\begin{array}{c|c}
7 & -3 \\
9 & -1 \\
\hline
6 & +3
\end{array}
\qquad \text{or} \qquad
\begin{array}{c|c}
7 & -3 \\
9 & -1 \\
\hline
6 & +3
\end{array}
$$

> **Note:** *RHB will always contain same number of digits as to number of zero in the nearest base of the given number.*

$$
\begin{array}{rr}
7 & -3 \\
9 & -1 \\
\hline
6 & |\ +3 \\
\end{array}
$$

$$7 \times 9 = 63$$

Let us now talk about the numbers which are near to base 100.

Example 4.8: 97×92.

Solution:

Step 1:   Near to base 100

Step 2:

$$
\begin{array}{rr}
97 & -03 \\
92 & -08 \\
\hline
\text{LHB} & |\ \text{RHB} \\
\end{array}
$$

Step 3:

$$
\begin{array}{rr}
97 & -03 \\
92 & -08 \\
\hline
\text{LHB} & |\ +24 \\
\end{array}
$$

Step 4:

$$
\begin{array}{rr}
97 & -03 \\
92 & -08 \\
\hline
89 & |\ +24 \\
89 & |\ 24 \\
\end{array}
$$

$$= 8924 \textbf{ Ans.}$$

Example 4.9: 89×85.

Solution:

Step 1:   Near to base 100

Step 2:

$$
\begin{array}{rr}
89 & -11 \\
85 & -15 \\
\hline
\text{LHB} & |\ \text{RHB} \\
\end{array}
$$

Step 3:

$$
\begin{array}{rr}
89 & -11 \\
85 & -15 \\
\hline
\text{LHB} & |\ +165 \\
\end{array}
$$

Step 4:

$$
\begin{array}{r|l}
89 & -11 \\
85 & -15 \\
\hline
74 & +165 \\
\hline
74 & 165 \\
75 & 65 \\
\end{array}
$$

= 7565 **Ans.**

Example 4.10: 93 × 80.

Solution:

Step 1:   Near to base 100

Step 2:

$$
\begin{array}{r|l}
93 & -07 \\
80 & -20 \\
\hline
\text{LHB} & \text{RHB} \\
\end{array}
$$

Step 3:

$$
\begin{array}{r|l}
93 & -07 \\
80 & -20 \\
\hline
\text{LHB} & +140 \\
\end{array}
$$

Step 4:

$$
\begin{array}{r|l}
93 & -07 \\
80 & -20 \\
\hline
73 & +140 \\
\hline
74 & 140 \\
74 & 40 \\
\end{array}
$$

= 7440 **Ans.**

Let us now talk about the numbers which are near to base 1000

Example 4.11: 997 × 992.

Solution:

Step 1:   Near to base 1000

Step 2:

$$
\begin{array}{r|l}
997 & -003 \\
992 & -008 \\
\hline
\text{LHB} & \text{RHB} \\
\end{array}
$$

Step 3:

$$997 \quad -003$$
$$992 \quad -008$$
$$\left.\begin{array}{l}\end{array}\right\} \times$$

$$\overline{\text{LHB} \mid +024}$$

Step 4:

$$997 \quad -003$$
$$992 \quad -008$$

$$\overline{989 \mid +024}$$

$$989 \mid 024$$

$$= 989024 \textbf{ Ans.}$$

Example 4.12: 993 × 985.

Solution:

Step 1:   Near to base 1000

Step 2:

$$993 \quad -007$$
$$985 \quad -015$$

$$\overline{\text{LHB} \mid \text{RHB}}$$

Step 3:

$$993 \quad -007$$
$$985 \quad -015$$
$$\left.\begin{array}{l}\end{array}\right\} \times$$

$$\overline{\text{LHB} \mid +105}$$

Step 4:

$$993 \quad -007$$
$$985 \quad -015$$

$$\overline{978 \mid +105}$$

$$= 978105 \textbf{ Ans.}$$

Exercise for Practice

Solve the following questions:

11.	89 × 98	**12.**	85 × 97
13.	91 × 96	**14.**	93 × 95
15.	97 × 92	**16.**	99 × 88
17.	988 × 997	**18.**	986 × 992
19.	996 × 985	**20.**	997 × 990

When one Number is above and another number is below the Base

Let us understand the concept by taking numbers which are near to base 10.

Example 4.13: Solve 13 × 9.

Solution:

Step 1:   Here the nearest base is 10.

Step 2:   Write down both the numbers one above the other and their differences with respect to the base on the right hand side with their respective signs as shown below

$$13 \quad +3 \ (+3 = 13 - 10)$$
$$9 \quad -1 \ (-1 = 9 - 10)$$

Step 3:   Draw a vertical line to divide the given space into 2 boxes, *i.e.*, LHB and RHB as shown below

$$
\begin{array}{c|c}
13 & +3 \\
9 & -1 \\
\hline
\text{LHB} & \text{RHB}
\end{array}
$$

Step 4:   The value of RHB can be calculated by multiplying the two numbers which are placed above the RHB as shown below

$$
\begin{array}{c|c}
13 & +3 \\
9 & -1 \\
\hline
\text{LHB} & -3
\end{array}
$$

Step 5:   The value of LHB can be calculated by adding any two numbers with sign diagonally as shown below

$$
\begin{array}{c|c}
13 & +3 \\
9 & -1 \\
\hline
12 & -3
\end{array}
\qquad \text{or} \qquad
\begin{array}{c|c}
13 & +3 \\
9 & -1 \\
\hline
12 & -3
\end{array}
$$

Note: *RHB will always contain same number of digits as to number of zero in the nearest base of the given number.*

$$\begin{array}{r|r} 13 & +3 \\ 9 & -1 \\ \hline 12 & -3 \end{array}$$

> **Note:** *Since RHB cannot be negative, so in order to make it positive we will borrow 1 from LHB (equivalent to 10 as the base is 10) and add it with RHB to get 10 + (–3) =7.*

$$\begin{array}{r|r} 13 & +3 \\ 9 & -1 \\ \hline 11 & 7 \end{array}$$

$$13 \times 9 = 117$$

Example 4.14: 97 × 108.

Solution:

Step 1: Near to base 100

Step 2:

$$\begin{array}{r|r} 97 & -03 \\ 108 & +08 \\ \hline LHB & RHB \end{array}$$

Step 3:

$$\begin{array}{r|r} 97 & -03 \\ 108 & +08 \\ \hline LHB & -24 \end{array} \bigg\} \times$$

Step 4:

$$\begin{array}{r|r} 97 & -03 \\ 108 & +08 \\ \hline 105 & -24 \\ 104 & 76 \end{array}$$

> **Note:** *Since RHB cannot be negative, so in order to make it positive we will borrow 1 from LHB (equivalent to 100 as the base is 100) and add it with RHB to get 100 + (–24) =76.*

$$= 10476 \textbf{ Ans.}$$

Example 4.15: 980 × 1005.

Solution:

Step 1: Near to base 1000

Step 2:

980	−020
1005	+005
LHB	RHB

Step 3:

980	−020
1005	+005
LHB	−100

Step 4:

980	−03
1005	+05
985	−100
985	−100

> **Note:** *Since RHB cannot be negative, so in order to make it positive we will borrow 1 from LHB (equivalent to 1000 as the base is 1000) and add it with RHB to get 1000 + (−100) = 900.*

= 984900 **Ans.**

Exercise for Practice

Solve the following questions:

21. 106 × 98   **22.** 101 × 96

23. 103 × 95   **24.** 107 × 92

25. 109 × 88   **26.** 1008 × 999

27. 1014 × 992   **28.** 1019 × 985

29. 1015 × 990   **30.** 1011 × 993

CROSSWISE MULTIPLICATION

This is a very easy method which follows a one line approach of crosswise Multiplication. This is a general method which can be applied for multiplying any 2 numbers.

Conventional Way	*Vedic Way*

```
        12345              12345
      × 54219             ×54219
   ───────────      ─────────────────────────────
    1 1 1 1 0 5     5│14│25│37│58│49│41│41│45
    1 2 3 4 5 ×           669333555
    2 4 6 9 0 × ×
    4 9 3 8 0 × × ×
  6 1 7 2 5 × × × ×
  ───────────
  6 6 9 3 3 3 5 5 5
```

There are various cases for multiplying various digits, some of them are discussed below

- ◆ 2 × 2 digit multiplication
- ◆ 3 × 3 digit multiplication
- ◆ 3 × 2 digit multiplication
- ◆ 4 × 4 digit multiplication
- ◆ 4 × 3 digit multiplication
- ◆ 5 × 5 digit multiplication

Case I: 2×2 Digit Multiplication

Example 4.16: 45 × 63.

Step 1: Write down both the numbers one above the other with same gap in between the 2 numbers as shown below

$$4 \quad 5$$

$$6 \quad 3$$

Step 2 : Calculate the total number of digits (for example, we have 2 numbers of 2 digit each, so total number of digits is 4).

Here we have drawn number of boxes which are in accordance with

Number of boxes = Number of digits – 1

Number of boxes = 4 – 1 = 3

$$
\begin{array}{cc}
4 & 5 \\
6 & 3 \\
\hline
\text{III} \mid \text{II} \mid \text{I}
\end{array}
$$

Step 3: We will move from right to left. To calculate the answer of box I, multiply the right most digits of both numbers as shown below:

$$
\begin{array}{cc}
4 & 5 \\
6 & 3 \\
\hline
\text{III} \mid \text{II} \mid 15
\end{array}
$$

Step 4: To calculate the answer of box II, multiply all the digits cross wisely as shown below.

$$
\begin{array}{cc}
4 & 5 \\
6 & 3 \\
\hline
\text{III} \mid 42 \mid 15
\end{array}
$$

(4×3) + (6×5)

Step 5: To calculate the answer of box III, multiply the left most digits of both the numbers as shown below:

$$
\begin{array}{cc}
4 & 5 \\
6 & 3 \\
\hline
24 \mid 42 \mid 15
\end{array}
$$

> **Note:** *In this method of Multiplication, each box contains only 1 digit and rest all of them are carried over to the subsequent left hand box.*

Step 6:

$$\begin{array}{cc} 4 & 5 \\ 6 & 3 \end{array}$$

$$24 \mid 42 \mid 15$$

$$24 \mid 42 \mid 15$$

$$24 \mid 43 \mid 5$$

$$24 \mid 43 \mid 5$$

$$28 \mid 3 \mid 5$$

$$= 2835 \textbf{ Ans.}$$

Example 4.17: 91×87.

Step 1:

$$\begin{array}{cc} 9 & 1 \\ 8 & 7 \end{array}$$

Step 2:   Number of Boxes = $4 - 1 = 3$

$$\begin{array}{c|c|c} 9 & 1 \\ 8 & 7 \\ \hline \text{III} & \text{II} & \text{I} \end{array}$$

Step 3:

$$\left. \begin{array}{cc} 9 & 1 \\ 8 & 7 \end{array} \right\} \times$$

$$\text{III} \mid \text{II} \mid 7$$

Step 4:

$$\begin{array}{c|c|c} 9 & 1 \\ 8 & 7 \\ \hline \text{III} & 71 & 7 \end{array}$$

$$\downarrow$$

$$(9 \times 7) + (8 \times 1)$$

Step 5:

$$\times \left\{ \begin{array}{cc} 9 & 1 \\ 8 & 7 \end{array} \right.$$

$$72 \mid 71 \mid 7$$

$$72 \mid 71 \mid 7$$

$$79 \mid 1 \mid 7$$

$$= 7917 \textbf{ Ans.}$$

Example 4.18: 98 × 36.

Step 1:

$$\begin{array}{cc} 9 & 8 \\ 3 & 6 \end{array}$$

Step 2: Number of Boxes = 4 − 1 = 3

$$\begin{array}{c|c|c} 9 & 8 & \\ 3 & 6 & \\ \hline \text{III} & \text{II} & \text{I} \end{array}$$

Step 3:

$$\left.\begin{array}{cc} 9 & 8 \\ 3 & 6 \end{array}\right\} \times$$

$$\begin{array}{c|c|c} \text{III} & \text{II} & 48 \end{array}$$

Step 4:

$$\begin{array}{cc} 9 & 8 \\ 3 & 6 \end{array}$$

$$\begin{array}{c|c|c} \text{III} & 78 & 48 \end{array}$$

$$\downarrow$$

$$(9\times6) + (8\times3)$$

Step 5:

$$\times\left\{\begin{array}{cc} 9 & 8 \\ 3 & 6 \end{array}\right.$$

$$\begin{array}{c|c|c} 27 & 78 & 48 \end{array}$$

$$\begin{array}{c|c|c} 27 & 78 & \mathbf{48} \end{array}$$

$$\begin{array}{c|c|c} 27 & \mathbf{82} & 8 \end{array}$$

$$\begin{array}{c|c|c} 27 & \mathbf{82} & 8 \end{array}$$

$$\begin{array}{c|c|c} 35 & 2 & 8 \end{array}$$

$$= 3528 \textbf{ Ans.}$$

Teacher: Tell me a sentence that starts with an "I".

Student: I is the ....

Teacher: Stop! Never put 'is' after an 'I'. Always put 'am' after an 'I'.

Student: Ok, I am the 9th letter of alphabet.

Case 2: 3×3 Digit Multiplication.

Example 4.19: 123 × 151.

Solution:

Step 1:

1   2   3

1   5   1

Step 2: Number of Boxes = 6 − 1 = 5

1   2   3

1   5   1

V	IV	III	II	I

Step 3: We will move from right to left

1   2   3

1   5   1

V	IV	III	II	3

Step 4: To calculate the answer of box II, multiply the digits which are circled as shown in fig.

1   2   3

1   5   1

V	IV	III	17	3

$$\downarrow$$

$$(2×1) + (3×5)$$

Step 5: To calculate the value of box III, multiply all the digits as shown below:

1   2   3

1   5   1

V	IV	14	17	3

$$\downarrow$$

$$(1×1) + (1×3) + (2×5)$$

Step 6: To calculate the value of box IV, multiply the circled digits as shown below:

$$
\begin{array}{ccc}
1 & 2 & 3 \\
1 & 5 & 1
\end{array}
$$

| V | 7 | 14 | 17 | 3 |

$(1\times5) + (2\times1)$

Step 7: To calculate the value of box V, multiply the left 2 digits as shown below:

$$
\left\{
\begin{array}{ccc}
1 & 2 & 3 \\
1 & 5 & 1
\end{array}
\right.
$$

| 1 | 7 | 14 | 17 | 3 |

Step 8:

| 1 | 7 | 14 | 17 | 3 |

| 1 | 7 | 15 | 7 | 3 |
| 1 | 8 | 5 | 7 | 3 |

= 18573 **Ans.**

Example 4.20: 243 × 521.

Solution:

Step 1: Number of Boxes = 6 − 1 = 5

$$
\begin{array}{ccc}
2 & 4 & 3 \\
5 & 2 & 1
\end{array}
$$

| V | IV | III | II | I |

Step 2:

$$
\left.
\begin{array}{ccc}
2 & 4 & 3 \\
5 & 2 & 1
\end{array}
\right\} \times
$$

| V | IV | III | II | 3 |

Step 3:

$$
\begin{array}{ccc}
2 & 4 & 3 \\
5 & 2 & 1
\end{array}
$$

| V | IV | III | 10 | 3 |

$(4\times1) + (3\times2)$

Step 4:

$$\begin{array}{ccc} 2 & 4 & 3 \\ 5 & 2 & 1 \end{array}$$

| V | IV | 25 | 10 | 3 |

$$\downarrow$$

$$(2\times1) + (3\times5) + (4\times2)$$

Step 5:

$$\begin{array}{ccc} 2 & 4 & 3 \\ 5 & 2 & 1 \end{array}$$

| V | 24 | 25 | 10 | 3 |

$$\downarrow$$

$$(2\times2) + (4\times5)$$

Step 6:

$$\times \left\{ \begin{array}{ccc} 2 & 4 & 3 \\ 5 & 2 & 1 \end{array} \right.$$

| 10 | 24 | 25 | 10 | 3 |

Step 7:

10 | 24 | 25 | 10 | 3

10 | 24 | 26 | 0 | 3

10 | 26 | 6 | 0 | 3

12 | 6 | 6 | 0 | 3

$$= 126603 \textbf{ Ans.}$$

Example 4.21: 672 × 910.

Solution:

Step 1: Number of Boxes = 6 − 1 = 5

$$\begin{array}{ccc} 6 & 7 & 2 \\ 9 & 1 & 0 \end{array}$$

| V | IV | III | II | I |

Step 2:

$$\left. \begin{array}{ccc} 6 & 7 & 2 \\ 9 & 1 & 0 \end{array} \right\} \times$$

| V | IV | III | II | 0 |

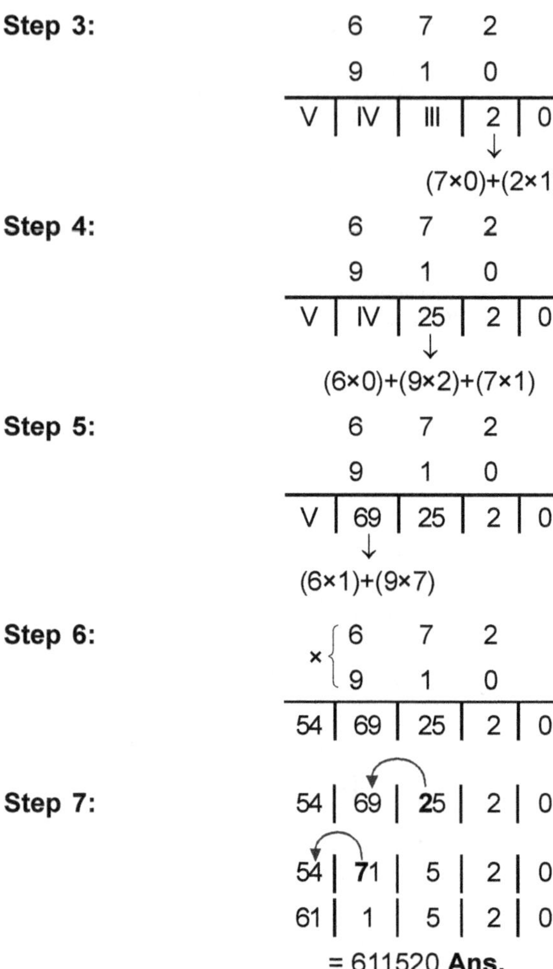

Case 3: 3×2 Digit Multiplication.

Example 4.22: 56 × 923.

Solution:

Step 1:   Just convert the 2 digit number into 3 digit number by adding a '0' from the left most side.

$$56 = 056$$

Now the question becomes 3 × 3 digit Multiplication.

Step 2:

	0	5	6	
	9	2	3	

V	IV	III	II	I

Step 3:

	0	5	6	
	9	2	3	

$\left. \begin{matrix} 6 \\ 3 \end{matrix} \right\} \times$

V	IV	III	II	18

Step 4:

	0	5	6
	9	2	3

V	IV	III	27	18

Step 5:

	0	5	6
	9	2	3

V	IV	64	27	18

Step 6:

	0	5	6
	9	2	3

V	45	64	27	18

Step 7:

	0	5	6
	9	2	3

0	45	64	27	18

Step 8:

0	45	64	27	**18**

0	45	64	**28**	8

0	45	**66**	8	8

0	**51**	6	8	8

5	1	6	8	8

= 51688 **Ans.**

Case 4: 4×4 Digit Multiplication.

Example 4.23: 1463 × 5218

Solution:

Step 1:   Total Number of Boxes = 8 − 1 = 7

	1	4	6	3
	5	2	1	8

VII	VI	V	IV	III	II	I

Step 2:

	1	4	6	3
	5	2	1	8

$$\left.\begin{array}{c} \end{array}\right\} \times$$

VII	VI	V	IV	III	II	24

Step 3:

	1	4	6	3
	5	2	1	8

$$\left.\begin{array}{c} \end{array}\right\} \times$$

VII	VI	V	IV	III	51	24

(8×6)+(3×1)

Step 4:

	1	4	6	3
	5	2	1	8

VII	VI	V	IV	44	51	24

(4×8)+(3×2)+(6×1)

Step 5:

	1	4	6	3
	5	2	1	8

VII	VI	V	39	44	51	24

(1×8)+(3×5)+(4×1)+(6×2)

Step 6:

	1	4	6	3
	5	2	1	8

VII	VI	39	39	44	51	24

(1×1)+(5×6)+(4×2)

Step 7:

$$\begin{array}{ccccccc} & 1 & & 4 & & 6 & & 3 \\ & 5 & & 2 & & 1 & & 8 \end{array}$$

| VII | 22 | 39 | 39 | 44 | 51 | 24 |

$(4×5)+(1×2)$

Step 8:

$$\times \begin{cases} 1 & 4 & 6 & 3 \\ 5 & 2 & 1 & 8 \end{cases}$$

| 5 | 22 | 39 | 39 | 44 | 51 | 24 |

Step 9:

| 5 | 22 | 39 | 39 | 44 | 51 | 24 |

| 5 | 22 | 39 | 39 | 44 | **53** | 4 |

| 5 | 22 | 39 | 39 | **49** | 3 | 4 |

| 5 | 22 | 39 | **43** | 9 | 3 | 4 |

| 5 | 22 | **43** | 3 | 9 | 3 | 4 |

| 5 | **26** | 3 | 3 | 9 | 3 | 4 |

| 7 | 6 | 3 | 3 | 9 | 3 | 4 |

$= 7633934$ **Ans.**

Boss: Where are you born?

Shyam: India.

Boss: Which Part?

Shyam: What 'which part?' whole body born in India.

Example 4.24: 9321 × 3123.

Solution:

Step 1:   Total Number of Boxes = 8 − 1 = 7

Step 2:

	9	3	2	1
	3	1	2	3

$\times$

VII	VI	V	IV	III	II	3

Step 3:

	9	3	2	1
	3	1	2	3

VII	VI	V	IV	III	8	3

$\downarrow$

$(2\times3)+(1\times2)$

Step 4:

	9	3	2	1
	3	1	2	3

VII	VI	V	IV	14	8	3

$\downarrow$

$(3\times3)+(1\times1)+(2\times2)$

Step 5:

	9	3	2	1
	3	1	2	3

VII	VI	V	38	14	8	3

$\downarrow$

$(9\times3)+(3\times1)+(3\times2)+(2\times1)$

Step 6:

	9	3	2	1
	3	1	2	3

VII	VI	27	38	14	8	3

$\downarrow$

$(9\times2)+(2\times3)+(3\times1)$

Step 7:

	9	3	2	1
	3	1	2	3

VII	18	27	38	14	8	3

$\downarrow$

$(9\times1)+(3\times3)$

Step 8:

$\times$

	9	3	2	1
	3	1	2	3

27	18	27	38	14	8	3

Step 9:

$$27 \mid 18 \mid 27 \mid 38 \mid 14 \mid 8 \mid 3$$

$$27 \mid 18 \mid 27 \mid 39 \mid 4 \mid 8 \mid 3$$

$$27 \mid 18 \mid 30 \mid 9 \mid 4 \mid 8 \mid 3$$

$$27 \mid 21 \mid 0 \mid 9 \mid 4 \mid 8 \mid 3$$

$$29 \mid 1 \mid 0 \mid 9 \mid 4 \mid 8 \mid 3$$

= 29109483 **Ans.**

Example 4.25: 9823 × 4351.

Solution:

Step 1:   Total Number of Boxes = 8 − 1 = 7

Step 2:

VII	VI	V	IV	III	II	3
9	8		2	3		
4	3		5	1		

$9 \quad 8 \quad 2 \quad 3 \Big\} \times$
$4 \quad 3 \quad 5 \quad 1$

Step 3:

$9 \quad 8 \quad 2 \quad 3$
$4 \quad 3 \quad 5 \quad 1$

VII	VI	V	IV	III	17	3

↓
(2×1) + (5×3)

Step 4:

$9 \quad 8 \quad 2 \quad 3$
$4 \quad 3 \quad 5 \quad 1$

VII	VI	V	IV	27	17	3

↓
(8×1)+(3×3)+(2×5)

Step 5:

$9 \quad 8 \quad 2 \quad 3$
$4 \quad 3 \quad 5 \quad 1$

VII	VI	V	67	27	17	3

↓
(9×1)+(3×4)+(8×5)+(2×)

Step 6:

$$
\begin{array}{ccccccc}
& 9 & 8 & 2 & 3 \\
& 4 & 3 & 5 & 1 \\
\hline
\text{VII} & \text{VI} & 77 & 67 & 27 & 17 & 3
\end{array}
$$

$\downarrow$

$(9\times5)+(2\times8)+(8\times3)$

Step 7:

$$
\begin{array}{ccccccc}
& 9 & 8 & 2 & 3 \\
& 4 & 3 & 5 & 1 \\
\hline
\text{VII} & 59 & 77 & 67 & 27 & 17 & 3
\end{array}
$$

$\downarrow$

$(9\times3)+(4\times8)$

Step 8:

$$
\times\begin{cases} 9 & 8 & 2 & 3 \\ 4 & 3 & 5 & 1 \end{cases}
$$

| 36 | 59 | 77 | 67 | 27 | 17 | 3 |

Step 9:

| 36 | 59 | 77 | 67 | 27 | **17** | 3 |

| 36 | 59 | 77 | 67 | **28** | 7 | 3 |

| 36 | 59 | 77 | **69** | 8 | 7 | 3 |

| 36 | 59 | **83** | 9 | 8 | 7 | 3 |

| 36 | **67** | 3 | 9 | 8 | 7 | 3 |

| 42 | 7 | 3 | 9 | 8 | 7 | 3 |

= 42739873 **Ans.**

Case 5: 4×3 Digit Multiplication.

Example 4.26: 9712 × 723.

Solution:

Step 1:   Convert the given 3 digit number (*i.e.*, 723) into 4 digit number by adding a zero from left most side.

723 = 0723

Step 2:   Total Number of Boxes = 8 – 1 = 7

		9	7	1	2
		0	7	2	3

VII	VI	V	IV	III	II	I

Step 3:

		9	7	1	2
		0	7	2	3

$\left. \begin{array}{c} \end{array} \right\} \times$

VII	VI	V	IV	III	II	6

Step 4:

		9	7	1	2
		0	7	2	3

VII	VI	V	IV	III	7	6

$\downarrow$

(1×3)+(2×2)

Step 5:

		9	7	1	2
		0	7	2	3

VII	VI	V	IV	37	7	6

$\downarrow$

(7×3) + (2×7) + (1×2)

Step 6:

		9	7	1	2
		0	7	2	3

VII	VI	V	48	37	7	6

$\downarrow$

(9×3)+(0×2)+(7×2)+(7×1)

Step 7:

		9	7	1	2
		0	7	2	3

VII	VI	67	48	37	7	6

$\downarrow$

(9×2) + (1×0) + (7×7)

Step 8:

		9	7	1	2
		0	7	2	3

VII	63	67	48	37	7	6

$\downarrow$

(9×7)+(7×0)

Step 9:

$$\times\begin{cases} 9 & 7 & 1 & 2 \\ 0 & 7 & 2 & 3 \end{cases}$$

$$0 \mid 63 \mid 67 \mid 48 \mid 37 \mid 7 \mid 6$$

Step 10:

$$0 \mid 63 \mid 67 \mid 48 \mid \mathbf{37} \mid 7 \mid 6$$

$$0 \mid 63 \mid 67 \mid \mathbf{51} \mid 7 \mid 7 \mid 6$$

$$0 \mid 63 \mid \mathbf{72} \mid 1 \mid 7 \mid 7 \mid 6$$

$$0 \mid \mathbf{70} \mid 2 \mid 1 \mid 7 \mid 7 \mid 6$$

$$7 \mid 0 \mid 2 \mid 1 \mid 7 \mid 7 \mid 6$$

$$= 7021776 \textbf{ Ans.}$$

Case 6: 5×5 Digit Multiplication.

Example 4.27: 97120 × 12723.

Solution:

Step 1:

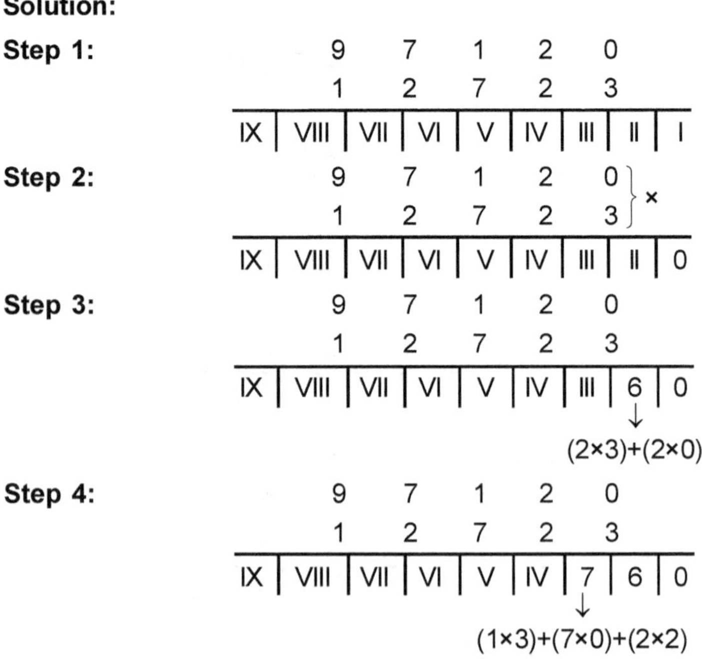

Step 2:

Step 3:

$(2\times3)+(2\times0)$

Step 4:

$(1\times3)+(7\times0)+(2\times2)$

Step 5:

		9	7	1	2	0		
		1	2	7	2	3		
IX	VIII	VII	VI	V	37	7	6	0

$$\downarrow$$
$$(7\times3)+(2\times0)+(1\times2)+(2\times7)$$

Step 6:

		9	7	1	2	0		
		1	2	7	2	3		
IX	VIII	VII	VI	52	37	7	6	0

$$\downarrow$$
$$(9\times3)+(1\times0)+(7\times2)+(2\times2)+(1\times7)$$

Step 7:

		9	7	1	2	0		
		1	2	7	2	3		
IX	VIII	VII	71	52	37	7	6	0

$$\downarrow$$
$$(9\times2)+(1\times2)+(7\times7)+(2\times1)$$

Step 8:

		9	7	1	2	0		
		1	2	7	2	3		
IX	VIII	78	71	52	37	7	6	0

$$\downarrow$$
$$(9\times7)+(1\times1)+(7\times2)$$

Step 9:

		9	7	1	2	0		
		1	2	7	2	3		
IX	25	78	71	52	37	7	6	0

$$\downarrow$$
$$(9\times2)+(7\times1)$$

Step 10:

		9	7	1	2	0		
		1	2	7	2	3		
9	25	78	71	52	37	7	6	0

Step 11:

$$9 \mid 25 \mid 78 \mid 71 \mid 52 \mid 37 \mid 7 \mid 6 \mid 0$$

$$9 \mid 25 \mid 78 \mid 71 \mid \mathbf{55} \mid 7 \mid 7 \mid 6 \mid 0$$

$$9 \mid 25 \mid 78 \mid \mathbf{76} \mid 5 \mid 7 \mid 7 \mid 6 \mid 0$$

$$9 \mid 25 \mid \mathbf{85} \mid 6 \mid 5 \mid 7 \mid 7 \mid 6 \mid 0$$

$$9 \mid \mathbf{33} \mid 5 \mid 6 \mid 5 \mid 7 \mid 7 \mid 6 \mid 0$$

$$12 \mid 3 \mid 5 \mid 6 \mid 5 \mid 7 \mid 7 \mid 6 \mid 0$$

= 1235657760 **Ans.**

Example 4.28: 82135 × 23657.

Solution:

Step 1:

| 8 | 2 | 1 | 3 | 5 |
| 2 | 3 | 6 | 5 | 7 |

}×

| IX | VIII | VII | VI | V | IV | III | II | I |

Step 2:

| 8 | 2 | 1 | 3 | 5 |
| 2 | 3 | 6 | 5 | 7 |

}×

| IX | VIII | VII | VI | V | IV | III | II | 35 |

Step 3:

| 8 | 2 | 1 | 3 | 5 |
| 2 | 3 | 6 | 5 | 7 |

| IX | VIII | VII | VI | V | IV | III | 46 | 35 |

$$\downarrow$$
$$(3\times7)+(5\times5)$$

Step 4:

| 8 | 2 | 1 | 3 | 5 |
| 2 | 3 | 6 | 5 | 7 |

| IX | VIII | VII | VI | V | IV | 52 | 46 | 35 |

$$\downarrow$$
$$(1\times7)+(5\times6)+(3\times5)$$

Step 5:

	8	2	1	3	5			
	2	3	6	5	7			
IX	VIII	VII	VI	V	52	52	46	35

$$\downarrow$$
$$(2\times7)+(5\times3)+(1\times5)+(3\times6)$$

Step 6:

	8	2	1	3	5			
	2	3	6	5	7			
IX	VIII	VII	VI	91	52	52	46	35

$$\downarrow$$
$$(8\times7)+(5\times2)+(2\times5)+(3\times3)+(1\times6)$$

Step 7:

	8	2	1	3	5			
	2	3	6	5	7			
IX	VIII	VII	61	91	52	52	46	35

$$\downarrow$$
$$(8\times5)+(3\times2)+(2\times6)+(1\times3)$$

Step 8:

	8	2	1	3	5			
	2	3	6	5	7			
IX	VIII	56	61	91	52	52	46	35

$$\downarrow$$
$$(8\times6)+(1\times2)+(2\times3)$$

Step 9:

	8	2	1	3	5			
	2	3	6	5	7			
IX	28	56	61	91	52	52	46	35

$$\downarrow$$
$$(8\times3)+(2\times2)$$

Step 10:

×	8	2	1	3	5			
	2	3	6	5	7			
16	28	56	61	91	52	52	46	35

Step 11:   16 | 28 | 56 | 61 | 91 | 52 | 52 | 46 | 35

                    16 | 28 | 56 | 61 | 91 | 52 | 52 | 49 | 5

                    16 | 28 | 56 | 61 | 91 | 52 | 56 | 9 | 5

                    16 | 28 | 56 | 61 | 91 | 57 | 6 | 9 | 5

                    16 | 28 | 56 | 61 | 96 | 7 | 6 | 9 | 5

                    16 | 28 | 56 | 70 | 6 | 7 | 6 | 9 | 5

                    16 | 28 | 63 | 0 | 6 | 7 | 6 | 9 | 5

                    16 | 34 | 3 | 0 | 6 | 7 | 6 | 9 | 5
                    19 | 4 | 3 | 0 | 6 | 7 | 6 | 9 | 5

                    = 1943067695 **Ans.**

Example 4.29: Multiply 12456 × 81236.

Solution:

	1	2	4	5	6			
	8	1	2	3	6			
8	17	36	51	73	40	51	48	36

= 1011875616 **Ans.**

Example 4.30: Multiply 32181 × 49712.

Solution:

	3	2	1	8	1			
	4	9	7	1	2			
12	35	43	58	91	70	17	17	2

= 1599781872 **Ans.**

Exercise for Practice

Solve the following questions:

31.	69 × 53	**32.**	77 × 81
33.	78 × 82	**34.**	55 × 62
35.	99 × 67	**36.**	98 × 32
37.	234 × 765	**38.**	987 × 126
39.	911 × 348	**40.**	881 × 467
41.	653 × 421	**42.**	786 × 654
43.	999 × 24	**44.**	987 × 43
45.	678 × 43	**46.**	762 × 87
47.	1236 × 9873	**48.**	9836 ×4376
49.	7623 × 2765	**50.**	1289 ×5342
51.	9832 × 675	**52.**	1239 × 234
53.	4674 × 875	**54.**	7324 × 876
55.	78541 × 34252	**56.**	95432 × 98656
57.	87543 × 89643	**58.**	87564 × 23548

MAGICAL SQUARES

A man found a cocoon of a butterfly. One day a small opening appeared. He sat and watched the butterfly for several hours as it struggled to squeeze its body through the tiny hole. Then it stopped, as if it couldn't go further.

So the man decided to help the butterfly. He took a pair of scissors and snipped off the remaining bits of cocoon. The butterfly emerged easily but it had a swollen body and shriveled wings.

The man continued to watch it, expecting that any minute the wings would enlarge and expand enough to support the body, neither happened! In fact the butterfly spent the rest of its life crawling around. It was never able to fly.

What the man in his kindness and haste did not understand: The restricting cocoon and the struggle required by the butterfly to get through the opening was a way of forcing the fluid from the body into the wings so that the wings would be ready for flight once that was achieved.

Sometimes struggles are exactly what we need in our lives. Going through life with no obstacles would cripple us. We will not be as strong as we could have been and we would never fly.

In General terms, squaring a number means multiplying the given number with itself. If you see the conventional way of finding the square of any given number, it is very boring and complex. The only way of finding the square is via Multiplication.

But this is not the case in Vedic Mathematics. In Vedic Mathematics anyone can find the square of any given number even without using pen and paper. But this can only be achieved with practice. There are various methods for finding the squares which are given below:

❖ **Finding Square of Numbers ending with 5.**

❖ **Finding Square of Numbers near to base.**

❖ **Finding Square of any Number.**

FINDING SQUARE OF NUMBERS ENDING WITH 5

Find 25²

Conventional Method	*Vedic Method*

$$2 \quad 5$$
$$\underline{2 \quad 5}$$
$$1 \quad 2 \quad 5$$
$$\underline{5 \quad 0 \quad \times}$$
$$6 \quad 2 \quad 5$$

Vedic Method:

$$2\,5^2 = 6 \mid 25$$

To find the answer of any such number we will create 2 boxes, *i.e.*, Left Hand Box (LHB) and Right Hand Box (RHB) by placing a vertical line in between as shown below:

Square of Number = LHB | RHB

Example 5.1: Find 25².

Solution:

Step 1: Simply draw 2 boxes, *i.e.*, LHB and RHB

$$25^2 = \text{LHB} \mid \text{RHB}$$

Step 2: In RHB, 25 will always come *(25 is the square of 5 which is the right digit of the given number).*

$$2\,5^2$$

$$25^2 = \text{LHB} \mid 25$$

Step 3: In LHB, the left digit of number (*i.e.*, 2 of 25) is multiplied with the next consecutive digit (which comes after it).

$$25^2 = 3 \times 2 \mid 25$$

Next consecutive digit which comes after 2   **Left digit of number**

$$25^2 = 06 \mid 25$$

625 is the square of 25.

> ***Zero is the only number which is known with so many names including nought, nil, zip etc.***

Example 5.2: Find 85^2.
Solution:

Step 1:	85^2 = LHB | RHB
Step 2:	85^2 = LHB | 25
Step 3:	85^2 = 9×8 | 25
	85^2 = 72 | 25 = 7225 **Ans.**

Example 5.3: Find 95^2.
Solution:

Step 1:	95^2 = LHB | RHB
Step 2:	95^2 = LHB | 25
Step 3:	95^2 = 10×9 | 25
	95^2 = 90 | 25
	95^2 = 9025 **Ans.**

Example 5.4: Find 125^2.
Solution:

Step 1:	125^2 = LHB | RHB
Step 2:	125^2 = LHB | 25
Step 3:	125^2 = 13×12 | 25
	125^2 = 156 | 25
	125^2 = 15625 **Ans.**

Exercise for Practice

Find the square of the following

1.	35	**2.**	45
3.	55	**4.**	65
5.	75	**6.**	105
7.	115	**8.**	135
9.	145	**10.**	155

SQUARE OF NUMBERS NEAR TO BASE

Base are the numbers which are formed with the help of 1 and 0. For example: 10, 100, 1000 etc.

Just like previous method of finding the squares, here also the answer will come in 2 boxes, *i.e.*, LHB and RHB. The formula for finding the square of numbers is

Square of Number = Number ± D | D²

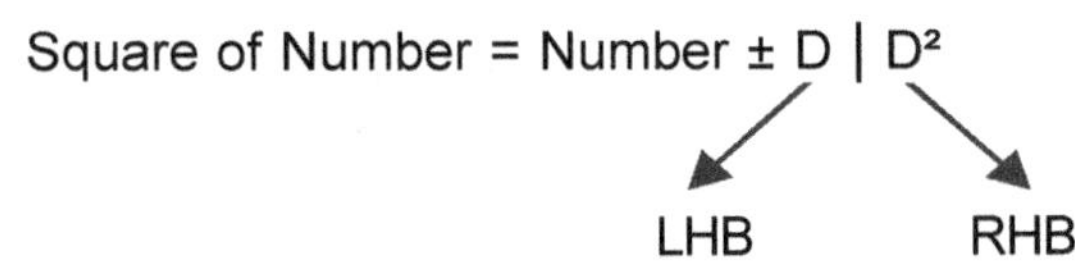

> **Note:** *Here D is Deficiency or Surplus. If the number is smaller than base (– ve) sign is used and if the number is bigger than base. (+ ve) sign is used from ±.*
>
> *RHB will always contain 2 digits.*

Let us understand it in a better way with the help of a solved example.

Example 5.5: Find 98².

Solution:

Step 1: First of all we will check whether the given number is smaller or bigger than the nearest base. After this we will calculate the value of D which is

D = NEAREST BASE – NUMBER

D = 100 – 98 = 02

Step 2: Simply draw 2 boxes i.e. LHB and RHB

98² = LHB | RHB

Step 3: The value of RHB is calculated below

RHB = D² = 2² = 04

98² = LHB | 04

Step 4: For the value of LHB, calculate it from the given formula

LHB = Number – D

(in case number is smaller than the base, we will use –)

$$LHB = 98 - 02 = 96$$

$$98^2 = LHB \mid 04$$

$$98^2 = 96 \mid 04$$

9604 is the square of **98.**

Example 5.6: Find 104^2.

Solution:

Step 1: First of all we will see the given number whether it is smaller or bigger than the nearest base. After this we will calculate the value of D which is

$$D = NEAREST\ BASE - NUMBER$$

$$D = 100 - 104 = \mid -04 \mid$$

Step 2: Draw 2 boxes *i.e.*, LHB and RHB

$$104^2 = LHB \mid RHB$$

Step 3: The value of RHB is calculated as:

$$RHB = D^2 = 04^2 = 16$$

$$104^2 = LHB \mid 16$$

Step 4: For the value of LHB, calculate it from the given formula

$$LHB = Number + D$$
(in case number is smaller than base, we will use +)

$$LHB = 104 + 04 = 108$$

$$104^2 = LHB \mid 16$$

$$104^2 = 108 \mid 16$$

10816 is the square of **104.**

> ***Mathematics is a great Motivator for all humans because its career starts from 'zero' but it goes on till 'infinity'.***

Example 5.7: Find 94^2.

Solution:

Step 1: $$D = 100 - 94 = 06$$

Step 2: 94^2 = LHB | RHB

Step 3:   RHB = D^2 = 06^2 = 36

                       94^2 = LHB | 36

Step 4:   LHB = 94 − 06 = 88

                       94^2 = 88 | 36

                       8836 is the square of **94**.

Example 5.8: Find 113^2.

Solution:

Step 1:   D = 100 − 113 = 13

Step 2: 113^2 = LHB | RHB

Step 3:   RHB = D^2 = 13^2 = 169

                       113^2 = LHB | 169

Step 4:   LHB = 113 + 13 = 126

                       113^2 = 126 | **1**69

                       113^2 = 127 | 69

                       12769 is the square of **113**.

Example 5.9: Find 108^2.

Solution:

Step 1:   D = 100 − 108 = | −08 |

Step 2: 108^2 = LHB | RHB

Step 3:   RHB = D^2 = 08^2 = 64

                       108^2 = LHB | 64

Step 4:   LHB = 108 + 08 = 116

                       108^2 = 11664

                       11664 is the square of **108**.

Exercise for Practice

Find the square of the following:

11.	79	**12.**	86
13.	89	**14.**	92
15.	94	**16.**	106
17.	109	**18.**	111
19.	114	**20.**	119

Son: "My Mathematics teacher is crazy".

Mother: "Why"?

Son: "Yesterday she told us that 5 is 4 + 1; today she is telling us that 5 is 3 + 2".

FINDING SQUARE OF ANY NUMBER

For finding the square of any given number we will follow the formula which is based on **Dvandva - Yoga** or **the Duplex Combination Process.**

For 2 Digit Numbers we use the following Formula

$$\text{Square} = a^2 \mid 2ab \mid b^2$$

If you see the above formula, it is just a modification of the given formula

$$(a + b)^2 = a^2 + 2ab + b^2$$

Just by replacing the + sign with a vertical line you get the ancient vedic method of finding the square of any give number.

$$\text{Square} = a^2 \mid 2ab \mid b^2$$

Example 5.9: Find 32^2.

Solution:

Step 1: Let us assume

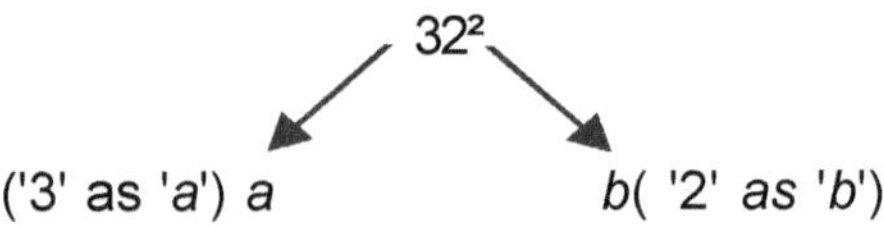

Step 2: Now putting the value of '*a*' and '*b*' in the given formula

$$32^2 = a^2 \mid 2ab \mid b^2$$

$$32^2 = 3^2 \mid 2 \times 3 \times 2 \mid 2^2$$

$$32^2 = 9 \mid 12 \mid 4$$

Step 3: Each box will contain only one digit and rest all extra digits will carry over to next box and we will do this while moving from right to left.

$$32^2 = 9 \mid 12 \mid 4$$

(Here 1 is carryover to right next box and added with 9)

$$32^2 = 10 \mid 2 \mid 4$$

1024 is the square of **32.**

From Number 0 to 1000, the letter 'A' only appears in 1000.

Example 5.10: Find 54^2.

Solution:

Step 1:

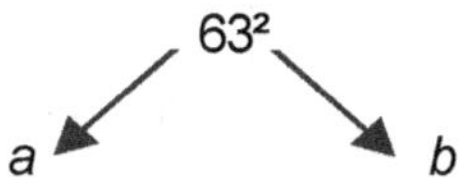

Step 2:

$54^2 = a^2 \mid 2ab \mid b^2$

$54^2 = 5^2 \mid 2{\times}5{\times}4 \mid 4^2$

$54^2 = 25 \mid 40 \mid 16$

Step 3:

$54^2 = 25 \mid 40 \mid \overset{\frown}{16}$

(Here 1 is carryover to right next box and added with 40)

$54^2 = 25 \mid \overset{\frown}{41} \mid 6$

(Here 4 is carryover to right next box and added with 25)

$54^2 = 29 \mid 1 \mid 6$

2916 is the square of **54.**

Example 5.11: Find 63^2.

Solution:

Step 1:

Step 2:

$63^2 = a^2 \mid 2ab \mid b^2$

$63^2 = 6^2 \mid 2{\times}6{\times}3 \mid 3^2$

$63^2 = 36 \mid 36 \mid 9$

Step 3:

$63^2 = 36 \mid \overset{\frown}{36} \mid 9$

$54^2 = 39 \mid 6 \mid 9$

3969 is the square of **63.**

Example 5.12: Find 71^2.

Solution:

Step 1:

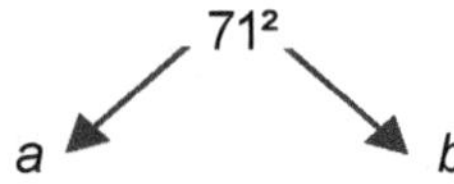

Step 2:

$71^2 = a^2 \mid 2ab \mid b^2$

$71^2 = 7^2 \mid 2 \times 7 \times 1 \mid 1^2$

$71^2 = 49 \mid 14 \mid 1$

Step 3:

$71^2 = 49 \mid 14 \mid 1$

$71^2 = 50 \mid 4 \mid 1$

5041 is the square of **71.**

Example 5.13: Find 76^2.

Solution:

Step 1:

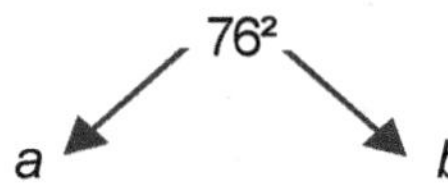

Step 2:

$76^2 = a^2 \mid 2ab \mid b^2$

$76^2 = 7^2 \mid 2 \times 7 \times 6 \mid 6^2$

$76^2 = 49 \mid 84 \mid 36$

Step 3:

$76^2 = 49 \mid 84 \mid 36$

$76^2 = 49 \mid 87 \mid 6$

$76^2 = 57 \mid 7 \mid 6$

5776 is the square of **76.**

Example 5.14: Find 83^2.

Solution:

Step 1:

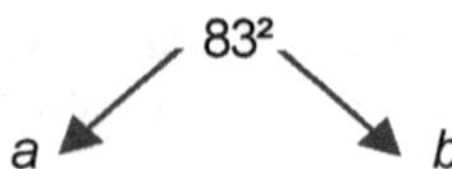

Step 2: $83^2 = a^2 \mid 2ab \mid b^2$

                            $83^2 = 8^2 \mid 2{\times}8{\times}3 \mid 3^2$

                            $83^2 = 64 \mid 48 \mid 9$

Step 3: $83^2 = 64 \mid \mathbf{48} \mid 9$

                            $83^2 = 68 \mid 8 \mid 9$

                            6889 is the square of **83**.

Example 5.15: Find 99^2.

Solution:

Step 1:

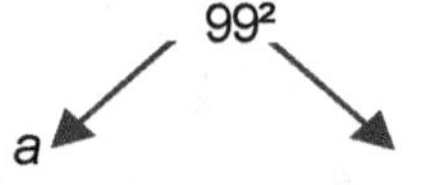

Step 2: $99^2 = a^2 \mid 2ab \mid b^2$

                            $99^2 = 9^2 \mid 2{\times}9{\times}9 \mid 9^2$

                            $99^2 = 81 \mid 162 \mid 81$

Step 3: $99^2 = 81 \mid 162 \mid \mathbf{81}$

                            $99^2 = 81 \mid \mathbf{170} \mid 1$

                            $99^2 = 98 \mid 0 \mid 1$

                            9801 is the square of **99**.

Example 5.16: Find 67^2.

Solution:

Step 1: $a = 6$ and $b = 7$

Step 2: $67^2 = 36 \mid 84 \mid 49$

Step 3: $67^2 = 44 \mid 8 \mid 9$

                            4489 is the square of **67**.

Example 5.17: Find 33^2.

Solution:

Step 1: $a = 3$ and $b = 3$

Step 2: $33^2 = 9 \mid 18 \mid 9$

Step 3: $33^2 = 10 \mid 8 \mid 9$

                  1089 is the square of **33**.

> ### *Go down deep enough into anything and you will find Mathematics.*

Example 5.18: Find 39^2.

Solution:

Step 1: $a = 3$ and $b = 9$

Step 2: $39^2 = 9 \mid 54 \mid 81$

Step 3: $39^2 = 15 \mid 2 \mid 1$

                  1521 is the square of **39**.

Example 5.19: Find 52^2.

Solution:

Step 1: $a = 5$ and $b = 2$

Step 2: $52^2 = 25 \mid 20 \mid 4$

Step 3: $52^2 = 27 \mid 0 \mid 4$

                  2704 is the square of **52**.

Example 5.20: Find 58^2.

Solution:

Step 1: $a = 5$ and $b = 8$

Step 2: $58^2 = 25 \mid 80 \mid 64$

Step 3: $58^2 = 33 \mid 6 \mid 4$

                  3364 is the square of **58**.

Example 5.21: Find 64^2.

Solution:

Step 1: $a = 6$ and $b = 4$

Step 2: $64^2 = 36 \mid 48 \mid 16$

Step 3: $\quad\quad\quad\quad\quad\quad$ $64^2 = 40 \mid 9 \mid 6$

$\quad\quad\quad\quad\quad\quad$ **4096** is the square of **64.**

Example 5.22: Find 71^2.

Solution:

Step 1: $\quad\quad\quad\quad\quad$ $a = 7$ and $b = 1$

Step 2: $\quad\quad\quad\quad\quad$ $71^2 = 49 \mid 14 \mid 1$

Step 3: $\quad\quad\quad\quad\quad$ $71^2 = 50 \mid 4 \mid 1$

$\quad\quad\quad\quad\quad\quad$ **5041** is the square of **71.**

Example 5.23: Find 79^2.

Solution:

Step 1: $\quad\quad\quad\quad\quad$ $a = 7$ and $b = 9$

Step 2: $\quad\quad\quad\quad\quad$ $79^2 = 49 \mid 126 \mid 81$

Step 3: $\quad\quad\quad\quad\quad$ $79^2 = 62 \mid 4 \mid 1$

$\quad\quad\quad\quad\quad\quad$ **6241** is the square of **79.**

Example 5.24: Find 85^2.

Solution:

Step 1: $\quad\quad\quad\quad\quad$ $a = 8$ and $b = 5$

Step 2: $\quad\quad\quad\quad\quad$ $85^2 = 64 \mid 80 \mid 25$

Step 3: $\quad\quad\quad\quad\quad$ $85^2 = 72 \mid 2 \mid 5$

$\quad\quad\quad\quad\quad\quad$ **7225** is the square of **85.**

Exercise for Practice

Find the square of the following

21.	53	**22.**	45
23.	67	**24.**	89
25.	91	**26.**	81
27.	87	**28.**	32
29.	97	**30.**	64

> **For 3 Digit Numbers we use the following Formula**

$$abc^2 = a^2 \mid 2ab \mid 2ac + b^2 \mid 2bc \mid c^2$$

Example 5.25: Find 123^2.

Solution:

Step 1:   Let us assume

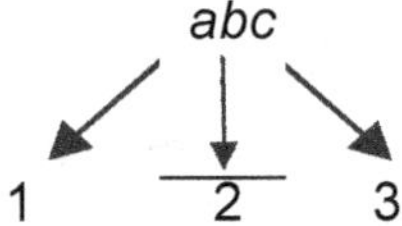

Step 2:   Putting the values of *a*, *b* and *c* in the given formula

$$123^2 = 1^2 \mid 2{\times}1{\times}2 \mid 2{\times}1{\times}3+2^2 \mid 2{\times}2{\times}3 \mid 3^2$$

$$123^2 = 1 \mid 4 \mid 10 \mid 12 \mid 9$$

Step 3:   Each box will contain only one digit and rest all extra digits will carry over to next box and we will do this while moving from right to left.

$$123^2 = 1 \mid 4 \mid 10 \mid 12 \mid 9$$

$$123^2 = 1 \mid 4 \mid 11 \mid 2 \mid 9$$

$$123^2 = 1 \mid 5 \mid 1 \mid 2 \mid 9$$

15129 is the square of **123**.

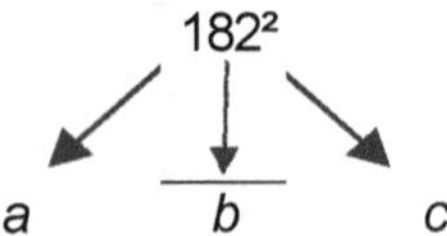

Teacher to Ravi : Ravi, I am glad to see your writing has improved!

Ravi : Thank you!

Teacher : Now, finally I can see how bad your spellings are?

Example 5.26: Find 182^2.

Solution:

Step 1:

Step 2: $182^2 = 1^2 \mid 2{\times}1{\times}8 \mid 2{\times}1{\times}2+8^2 \mid 2{\times}8{\times}2 \mid 2^2$

                     $182^2 = 1 \mid 16 \mid 68 \mid 32 \mid 4$

Step 3: $182^2 = 1 \mid 16 \mid 68 \mid 32 \mid 4$

                     $182^2 = 1 \mid 16 \mid 71 \mid 2 \mid 4$

                     $182^2 = 1 \mid 23 \mid 1 \mid 2 \mid 4$

                     $182^2 = 3 \mid 3 \mid 1 \mid 2 \mid 4$

               33124 is the square of **182.**

Example 5.27: Find 221^2.

Solution:

Step 1:

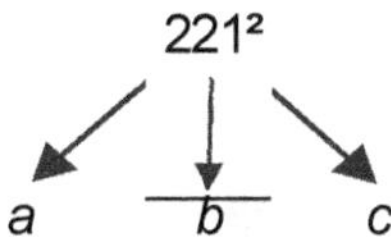

Step 2: $221^2 = 2^2 \mid 2{\times}2{\times}2 \mid 2{\times}2{\times}1+2^2 \mid 2{\times}2{\times}1 \mid 1^2$

               $221^2 = 4 \mid 8 \mid 8 \mid 4 \mid 1$

               $221^2 = 48841$ **Ans.**

Example 5.28: Find 314^2.

Solution:

Step 1:

Step 2: $314^2 = 3^2 \mid 2{\times}3{\times}1 \mid 2{\times}3{\times}4+1^2 \mid 2{\times}1{\times}4 \mid 4^2$

               $314^2 = 9 \mid 6 \mid 25 \mid 8 \mid 16$

Step 3: $314^2 = 9 \mid 6 \mid 25 \mid 8 \mid 16$

               $314^2 = 9 \mid 6 \mid 25 \mid 9 \mid 6$

$$314^2 = 9 \mid 8 \mid 5 \mid 9 \mid 6$$

$$314^2 = 9 \mid 8 \mid 5 \mid 9 \mid 6$$

98596 is the square of **314.**

Example 5.29: Find 410^2.

Solution:

Step 1:

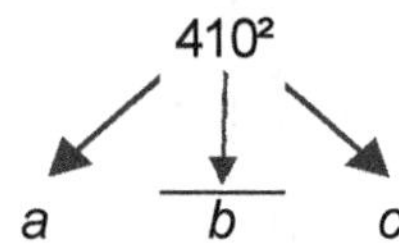

Step 2:

$$410^2 = 4^2 \mid 2{\times}4{\times}1 \mid 2{\times}4{\times}0{+}1^2 \mid 2{\times}1{\times}0 \mid 0^2$$

$$182^2 = 16 \mid 8 \mid 1 \mid 0 \mid 0$$

168100 is the square of **410.**

Exercise for Practice

Find the square of the following:

31.	153	**32.**	245
33.	671	**34.**	909
35.	191	**36.**	581
37.	807	**38.**	325
39.	812	**40.**	923

PAINLESS CUBES

Thousands of years ago in a small Italian town, a merchant had the misfortune of owing a large sum of money to a moneylender. The moneylender, who was old and ugly, fancied the merchant's beautiful daughter so he proposed a bargain. He said he would forgo the merchant's debt if he could marry the daughter to him. Both the merchant and his daughter were horrified by the proposal.

The moneylender gave them another proposal. He told them that he would put a black pebble and a white pebble into an empty bag. The girl would then have to pick one pebble from the bag. If she picked the black pebble, she would become the moneylender's wife and her father's debt would be forgiven. If she picked the white pebble she need not marry him and her father's debt would still be forgiven. But if she refused to pick a pebble, her father would be thrown into jail.

They were standing on a pebble strewn path in the moneylender's garden. As they talked, the moneylender bent over to pick up two pebbles. As he picked them up, the sharp-eyed girl noticed that he had picked up two black pebbles and put them into the bag. He then asked the girl to pick her pebble from the bag.

What would have you done if you were the girl? If you had to advise her, what would have been your advice? Careful analysis would produce three possibilities:

1. The girl should refuse to take a pebble.
2. The girl should show that there were two black pebbles in the bag and expose the moneylender as a cheat.

> *3. The girl should pick a black pebble and sacrifice herself in order to save her father from his debt and imprisonment.*
>
> *The above story is used with the hope that it will make us appreciate the difference between lateral and logical thinking.*
>
> *The girl put her hand into the moneybag and drew out a pebble. Without looking at it, she fumbled and let it fall onto the pebble-strewn path where it immediately became lost among all the other pebbles.*
>
> *"Oh, how clumsy of me," she said. "But never mind, if you look into the bag for the one that is left, you will be able to tell which pebble I picked." Since the remaining pebble was black, it was assumed that she had picked the white one. And since the moneylender dared not admit his dishonesty, the girl changed what seemed an impossible situation into an advantageous one.*
>
> *MORAL OF THE STORY: Most complex problems do have a solution, sometimes we have to think about them in a different way.*

Finding Cube of any given number is very tedious as one has to multiply the number 3 times. The only way to find out the cube in Conventional Method is through Multiplication. But the process of finding cube with the help of Vedic Mathematics is very easy and you can get the answer in only 2 lines.

The formula which is used to find out the cubes is just the modification of $(a + b)^3$ which is

$$(a + b)^3 = a^3 + 3a^2b + 3ab^2 + b^3$$

Now replacing '+' sign with ' | '(vertical lines) to convert it into 4 boxes.

$$(a + b)^3 = a^3 \mid 3a^2b \mid 3ab^2 \mid b^3$$

For finding the cube of any 2 digit number, just learn the cubes of the following

Numbers	*Cubes*
1	1
2	8
3	27

4	64
5	125
6	216
7	343
8	512
9	729

Now let us understand the given method with the help of Examples.

Example 6.1: Find the cube of 11.

Solution:

Step 1: Let us assume

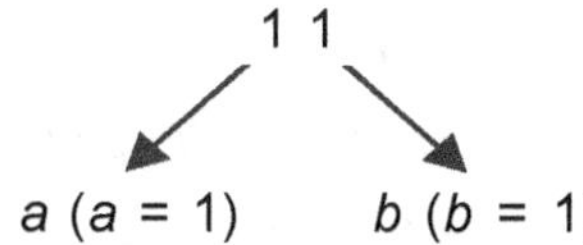

Step 2: Putting the values of a and b in the formula

$$(a+b)^3 = a^3 \mid 3a^2b \mid 3ab^2 \mid b^3$$

$$(11)^3 = 1^3 \mid 3(1)^2(1) \mid 3(1)(1)^2 \mid (1)^3$$

$$11^3 = 1 \mid 3 \mid 3 \mid 1$$

$$11^3 = 1331 \textbf{ Ans.}$$

Example 6.2: Find the cube of 13

Solution:

Step 1: Let us assume

1 3
a (a = 1) b (b = 3)

Step 2: Replacing the values of a and b in the formula

$$(a + b)^3 = a^3 \mid 3a^2b \mid 3ab^2 \mid b^3$$

$$(1 \mid 3)^3 = (1)^3 \mid 3(1)^2(3) \mid 3(1)(3)^2 \mid (3)^3$$

$$(1 \mid 3)^3 = 1 \mid 9 \mid 27 \mid 27$$

Step 3: $(1 \mid 3)^3 = 1 \mid 9 \mid 27 \mid 27$

$(1 \mid 3)^3 = 1 \mid 9 \mid 29 \mid 7 \Rightarrow = 1/0$

$(1 \mid 3)^3 = 1 \mid 11 \mid 9 \mid 7$

$(1 \mid 3)^3 = 2 \mid 1 \mid 9 \mid 7$

$13^3 = 2197$ **Ans.**

In an Interview,

Interviewer: How does an electric motor run?

Engineer: Dhhuuuurrrr.

Interviewer Shouts: Stop it.

Engineer: Dhuuurrr dhup dhup dhup.

Example 6.3: Find the cube of 22.

Solution:

Step 1:   Let us assume

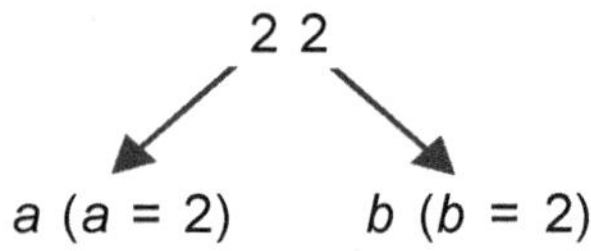

$a\ (a = 2)$ $b\ (b = 2)$

Step 2:   Replacing the values of a and b in the formula

$(a + b)^3 = a^3 \mid 3a^2b \mid 3ab^2 \mid b^3$

$(2 \mid 2)^3 = (2)^3 \mid 3(2)^2(2) \mid 3(2)(2)^2 \mid (2)^3$

$(2 \mid 2)^3 = 8 \mid 24 \mid 24 \mid 8$

Step 3: $(2 \mid 2)^3 = 8 \mid 24 \mid 24 \mid 8$

$(2 \mid 2)^3 = 8 \mid 26 \mid 4 \mid 8$

$(2 \mid 2)^3 = 10 \mid 6 \mid 4 \mid 8$

$22^3 = 10648$ **Ans.**

Example 6.4: Find the cube of 34.

Solution:

Step 1: Let us assume

$$3\ 4$$

$$a\ (a = 3) \qquad b\ (b = 4)$$

Step 2: Replacing the values of a and b in the formula

$$(a + b)^3 = a^3 \mid 3a^2b \mid 3ab^2 \mid b^3$$

$$(3 \mid 4)^3 = (3)^3 \mid 3(3)^2(4) \mid 3(3)(4)^2 \mid (4)^3$$

$$(3 \mid 4)^3 = 27 \mid 108 \mid 144 \mid 64$$

Step 3:

$$(3 \mid 4)^3 = 27 \mid 108 \mid 144 \mid \mathbf{64}$$

$$(3 \mid 4)^3 = 27 \mid 108 \mid \mathbf{150} \mid 4$$

$$(3 \mid 4)^3 = 27 \mid \mathbf{123} \mid 0 \mid 4$$

$$(3 \mid 4)^3 = 39 \mid 3 \mid 0 \mid 4$$

$$34^3 = 39304 \textbf{ Ans.}$$

Example 6.5: Find the cube of 47.

Solution:

Step 1: Let us assume

$$4\ 7$$

$$a\ (a = 4) \qquad b\ (b = 7)$$

Step 2: Replacing the values of a and b in the formula

$$(a + b)^3 = a^3 \mid 3a^2b \mid 3ab^2 \mid b^3$$

$$(4 \mid 7)^3 = (4)^3 \mid 3(4)^2(7) \mid 3(4)(7)^2 \mid (7)^3$$

$$(4 \mid 7)^3 = 64 \mid 336 \mid 558 \mid 343$$

Step 3: $(4 \mid 7)^3 = 64 \mid 336 \mid 588 \mid \mathbf{343}$

                       $(4 \mid 7)^3 = 64 \mid 336 \mid \mathbf{622} \mid 3$

                       $(4 \mid 7)^3 = 64 \mid \mathbf{398} \mid 2 \mid 3$

                       $(4 \mid 7)^3 = 103 \mid 8 \mid 2 \mid 3$

                       $47^3 = 103823$ Answer

Example 6.6: Find the cube of 61.

Solution:

Step 1:   Let us assume

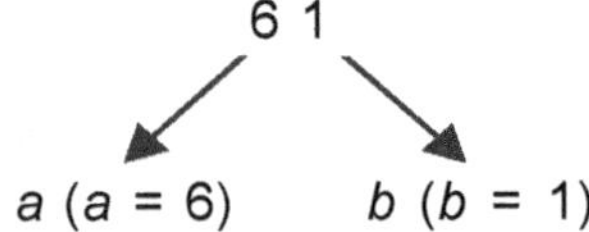

Step 2:   Replacing the values of *a* and *b* in the formula

               $(a + b)^3 = a^3 \mid 3a^2b \mid 3ab^2 \mid b^3$

               $(6 \mid 1)^3 = (6)^3 \mid 3(6)^2(1) \mid 3(6)(1)^2 \mid (1)^3$

               $(6 \mid 1)^3 = 216 \mid 108 \mid 18 \mid 1$

Step 3: $(6 \mid 1)^3 = 216 \mid 108 \mid \mathbf{18} \mid 1$

               $(6 \mid 1)^3 = 216 \mid \mathbf{109} \mid 8 \mid 1$

               $(6 \mid 1)^3 = 226 \mid 9 \mid 8 \mid 1$

               $61^3 = 226981$ **Ans.**

Example 6.7: Find the cube of 85.

Solution:

Step 1:   Let us assume

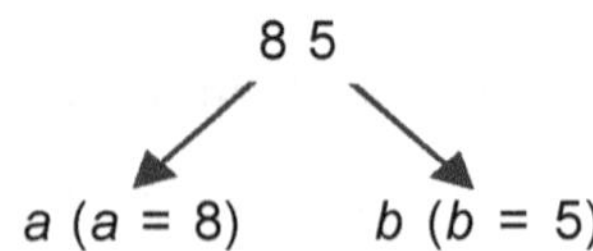

Step 2:   Replacing the values of a and b in the formula

$$(a + b)^3 = a^3 \mid 3a^2b \mid 3ab^2 \mid b^3$$

$$(8 \mid 5)^3 = (8)^3 \mid 3(8)^2(5) \mid 3(8)(5)^2 \mid (5)^3$$

$$(8 \mid 5)^3 = 512 \mid 960 \mid 600 \mid 125$$

Step 3: $(8 \mid 5)^3 = 512 \mid 960 \mid 600 \mid \mathbf{125}$

$$(8 \mid 5)^3 = 512 \mid 960 \mid \mathbf{612} \mid 5$$

$$(8 \mid 5)^3 = 512 \mid \mathbf{1021} \mid 2 \mid 5$$

$$(8 \mid 5)^3 = 614 \mid 1 \mid 2 \mid 5$$

$$85^3 = 614125 \text{ Answer}$$

Example 6.8: Find the cube of 93.

Solution:

Step 1:   Let us assume

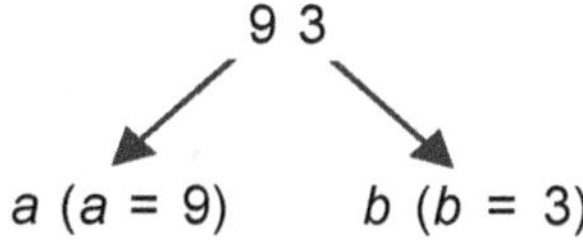

Step 2:   Replacing the values of a and b in the formula

$$(a + b)^3 = a^3 \mid 3a^2b \mid 3ab^2 \mid b^3$$

$$(9\ 3)^3 = (9)^3 \mid 3(9)^2(3) \mid 3(9)(3)^2 \mid (3)^3$$

$$(9 \mid 3)^3 = 729 \mid 729 \mid 243 \mid 27$$

Step 3: $(9 \mid 3)^3 = 729 \mid 729 \mid 243 \mid \mathbf{27}$

$$(9 \mid 3)^3 = 729 \mid 729 \mid \mathbf{245} \mid 7$$

$$(9 \mid 3)^3 = 729 \mid \mathbf{753} \mid 5 \mid 7$$

$$(9 \mid 3)^3 = 804 \mid 3 \mid 5 \mid 7$$

$$93^3 = 804357 \textbf{ Ans.}$$

SOME MORE SOLVED EXAMPLES

Example 6.9: Find 71^3.

$$71^3 = 7^3 \mid 3(7)^2(1) \mid 3(7)(1)^2 \mid 1^3$$

$$71^3 = 343 \mid 147 \mid 21 \mid 1$$

$$71^3 = 357911 \textbf{ Ans.}$$

Example 6.10: Find 91^3.

$$91^3 = 9^3 \mid 3(9)^2(1) \mid 3(9)(1)^2 \mid 1^3$$

$$91^3 = 729 \mid 243 \mid 27 \mid 1$$

$$91^3 = 753571 \textbf{ Ans.}$$

Exercise for Practice

Find the Cubes of the following

1.	23	**2.**	55
3.	37	**5.**	89
5.	41	**7.**	71
7.	27	**9.**	52
9.	99	**10.**	76

FRIENDLY DIVISION

A kindergarten teacher decided to let her class play a game. The teacher told the class, "You have to bring a plastic bag containing a few potatoes. Each potato will be given a name of person whom you hate. So the number of potatoes that you will put in the plastic bag will depend on the number of people you hate."

So when the day came, every child brought some potatoes with the name of the person(s) he/she hated. Some had 2 potatoes; some 3 while some up to 5 potatoes. The teacher then told the children to carry with them the potatoes in the plastic bag wherever they go (even to the toilet) for 1 week.

Days after days passed by, and the children started to complain due to the unpleasant smell let out by the rotten potatoes. Besides, those having 5 potatoes also had to carry heavier bags. After 1 week, the children were relieved because the game had finally ended....

The teacher asked: "How did you feel while carrying the potatoes with you for 1 week?" The children let out their frustrations and started complaining of the trouble that they had to go through having to carry the heavy and smelly potatoes wherever they went.

Then the teacher told them the hidden meaning behind the game. The teacher said: "This is exactly the situation when you carry your hatred for somebody inside your heart. The stench of hatred will contaminate your heart and you will carry it with you wherever you go. If you

> *cannot tolerate the smell of rotten potatoes for just 1 week, can you imagine what it is like to have the stench of hatred in your heart for your lifetime???"*
>
> *Moral of the story: Throw away any hatred from your heart. Forgiving others is the best attitude to take.*

For the numbers which are close to bases, we simply follow a base method of division or in Vedic language; we can say that we follow the Nikhilam Method (this method suggests that subtraction of all from 9 and of the last from 10).

Some General Guidelines:

There are basically 4 unique terms in Division, i.e., Divisor, Dividend, Quotient and Remainder. It is very important to understand it clearly which term represents what. I have tried to draw a pictorial representation

```
                          Dividend
                             |
                             ↓
        Divisor ←— 7 | 98 | 76 |
        Quotient ←—1410 | 6 —→ Remainder
```

- Now it is very important to identify the base which is close to Quotient. For example:

8	10 (10 − 2)
9	10 (10 − 1)
11	10 (10 + 1)
12	10 (10 + 2)
13	10 (10 + 3)
97	100 (100 − 03)
98	100 (100 − 02)
99	100 (100 − 01)
103	100 (100 + 03)
108	100 (100 + 08)
109	100 (100 + 09)

- After identifying the base, we need to check whether the Quotient is above the base or below the base. In both the cases, write down the difference with modulus.

- Depending upon the base we will divide the given Dividend in two different boxes such that the number of digits in the right hand box should be equal to the number of zeros in the base.

Teacher:	Who is your favourite author?
Pupil:	Salman Khan.
Teacher:	But Salman Khan never wrote any book.
Pupil:	You got it.

Example 7.1: 316/8.

Solution:

Step 1: Write down the question in the given form.

$$8 \lfloor 31 \lfloor 6 \lfloor 2$$

Step 2: Now simply write down the left most digit of left hand box to give the first digit of Quotient.

$$8 \lfloor 31 \lfloor 6 \lfloor 2$$
$$3$$

Step 3: Now multiply the Quotient digit (i.e., 3) with the difference of Divisor and Base (i.e., 2) and write it down below 1 as shown below

$$8 \lfloor 31 \mid 6 \lfloor 2$$
$$6$$
$$37 \quad (\times)$$

Step 4: Now we have 2 digits of Quotient with us which is 37.

Step 5: Now Multiply the Right most digit of Quotient with the difference and write it down below Right hand box as shown below:

$$8 \lfloor 31 \lfloor 6 \lfloor 2$$
$$14$$
$$37 \lfloor 20 \longrightarrow \text{Can further be divided}$$

Now since the remainder (i.e., 20) we get is greater than divisor, so we can further divide it.

Step 6:   After dividing 20 by 8, we get 2 as Quotient and 4 as Remainder. Now we will simply add this Quotient with the original Quotient to give final Quotient as

37 + 2 = 39

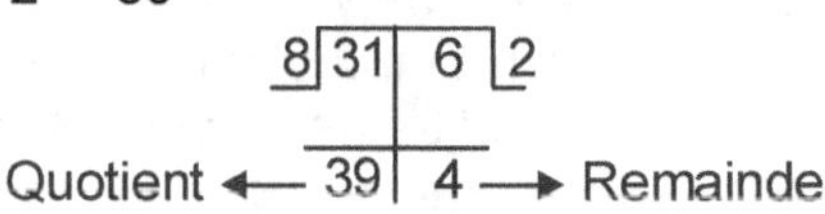

So now we have final equation with us which can be written as below:

Quotient = 39

Remainder = 4

Example 7.2: 509/9.

Solution:

Step 1:

Step 2:

Step 3:

Step 4:

Step 5:

Can further be divided

Step 6:

Example 7.3: 97/7.

Solution:

Step 1:

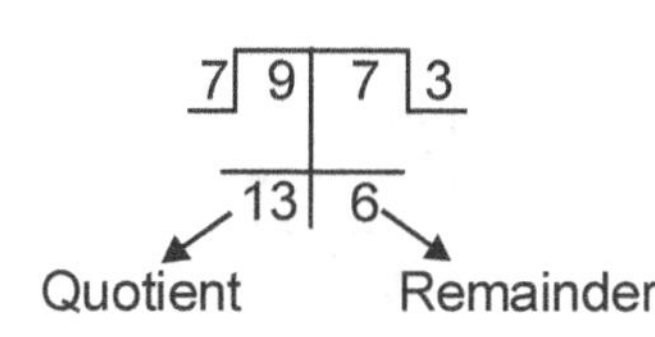

Step 2:

Step 3:

Quotient   Remainder

Example 7.4: 981/6.

Solution:

Step 1:

Step 2:

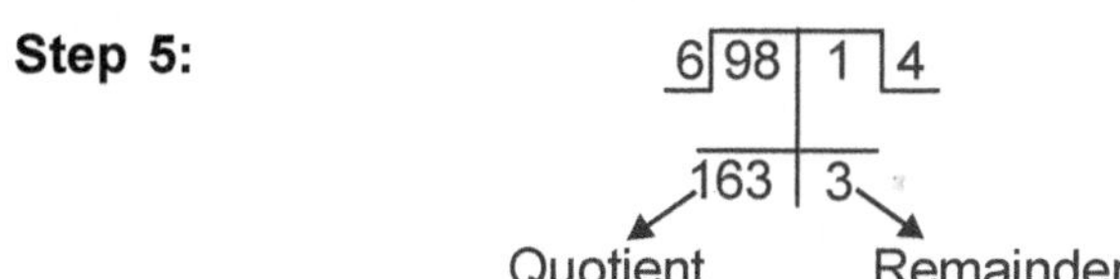
Can further be divided

Step 3:

6 | 98 | 1 | 4
162 | (×)

Step 4:

6 | 98 | 1 | 4
8
162 | 9

Step 5:

6 | 98 | 1 | 4
163 | 3
Quotient   Remainder

Teacher:	Where is Paris?
Student:	I don't know?
Teacher:	Where is Delhi?
Student:	I don't know?
Teacher:	Look then up in your book.
Student:	I don't know where that is, either.

Example 7.5: 683/7.

Solution:

Step 1:

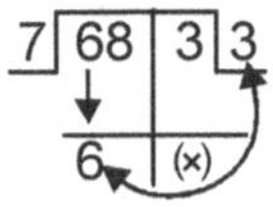

Step 2:

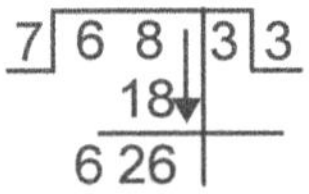

Step 3:

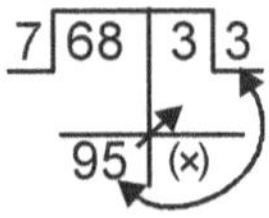

Step 4:

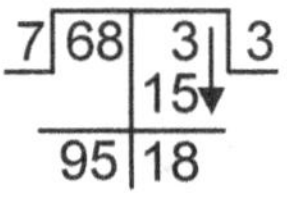

Step 5:

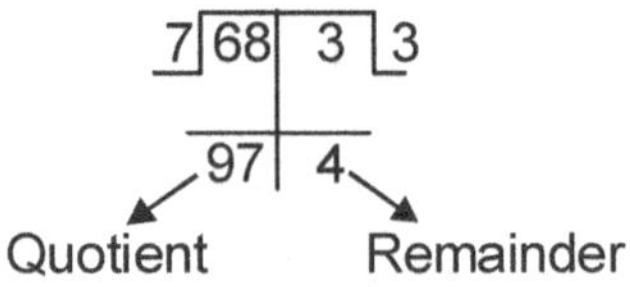

Quotient   Remainder

Example 7.6: 981/9.

Solution:

Step 1:

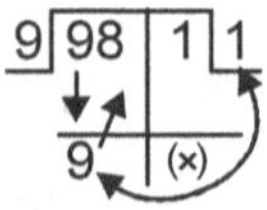

Step 2:

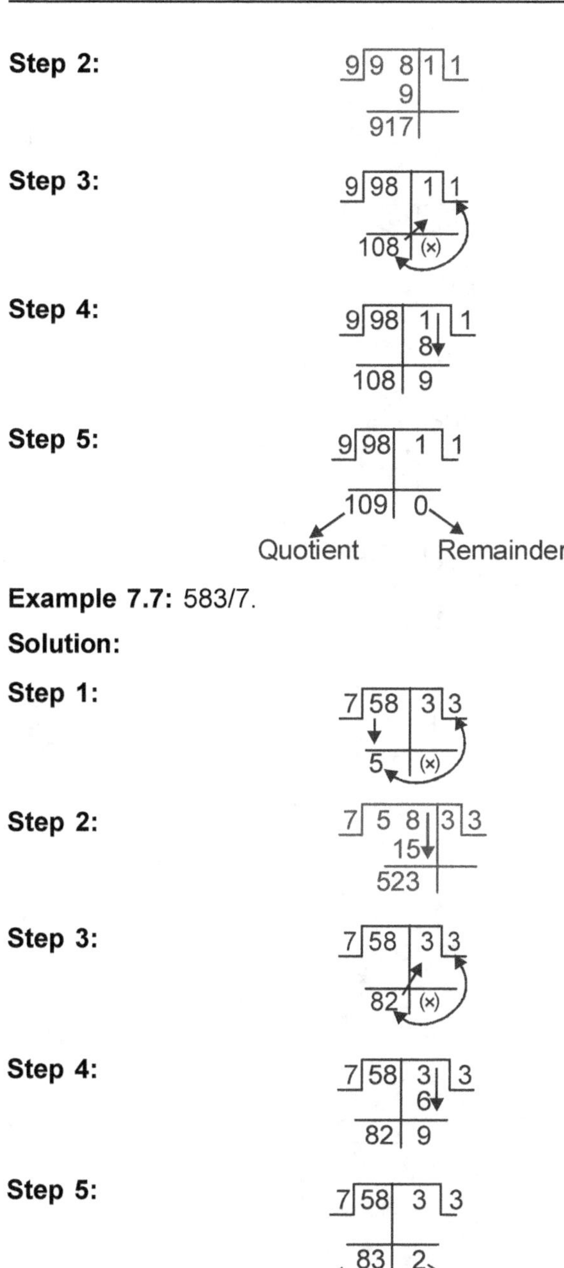

Step 3:

Step 4:

Step 5:

Quotient   Remainder

Example 7.7: 583/7.

Solution:

Step 1:

Step 2:

Step 3:

Step 4:

Step 5:

Quotient   Remainder

Example 7.8: 687/5.

Solution:

Step 1:

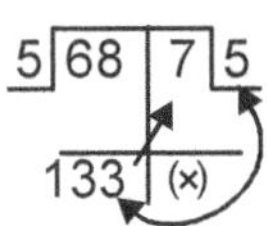

Step 2:

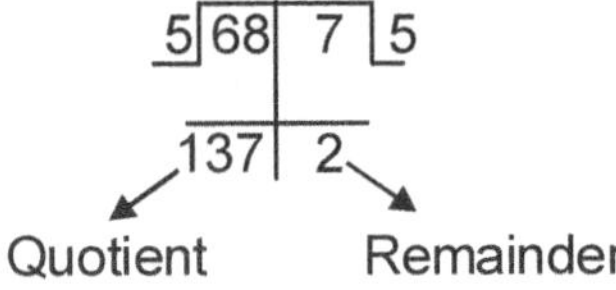

Step 3:

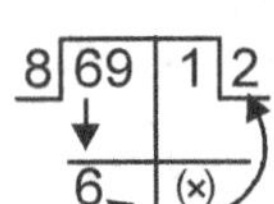

Step 4:

5|68| 7| 5
         15↓
133|22

Step 5:

5|68| 7| 5

137| 2

Quotient   Remainder

Example 7.9: 691/8.

Solution:

Step 1:

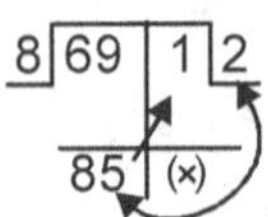

Step 2:

8| 6 9| 1| 2
        12↓
621

Step 3:

8|69| 1| 2

85| (×)

Step 4:

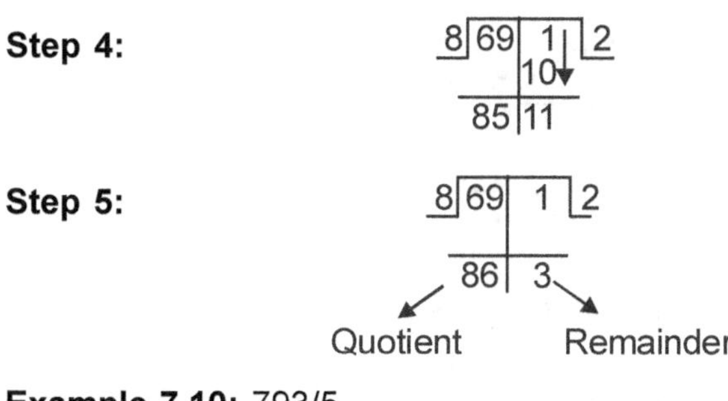

Step 5:

Quotient   Remainder

Example 7.10: 793/5.

Solution:

Step 1:

Step 2:

Step 3:

Step 4:

Step 5:

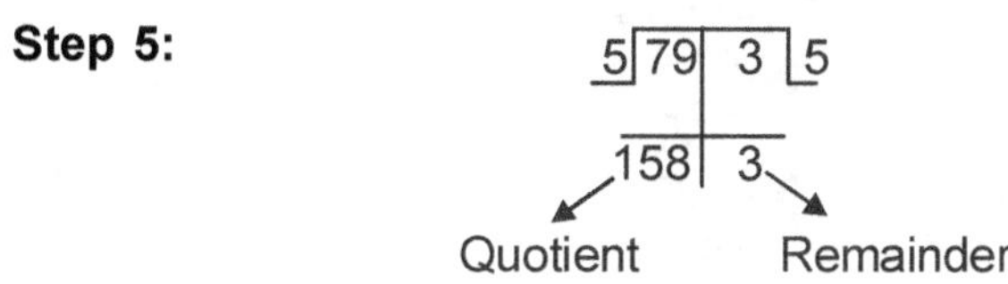

Quotient   Remainder

Example 7.11: 2403/96.

Solution:

Step 1:

Step 2:

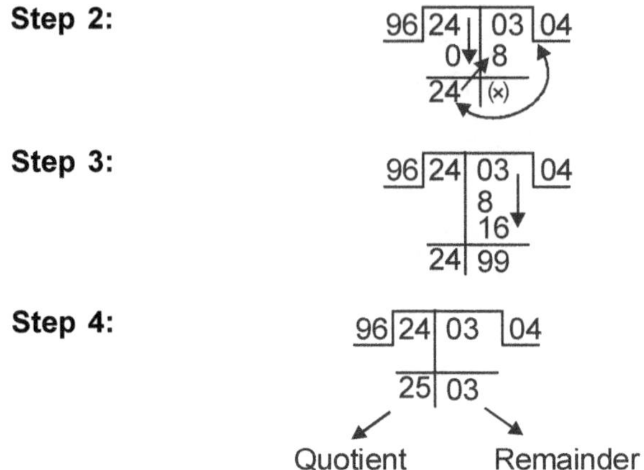

Step 3:

Step 4:

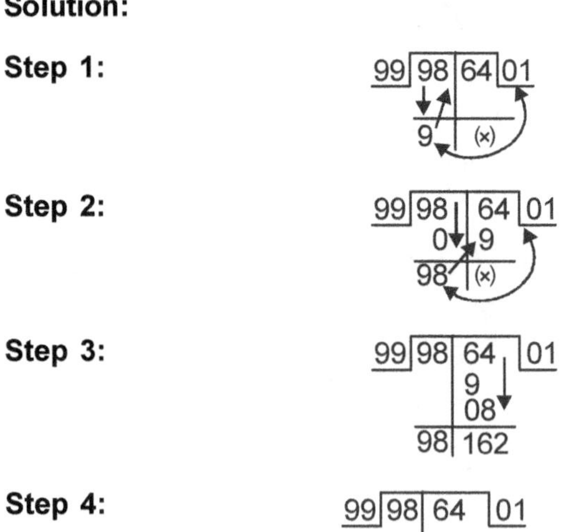

Quotient   Remainder

| Teacher: | Tell the class what book you read & what you thought of it. |
| Student: | I read phone book, but I didn't understand it. It had too many character. |

Example 7.12: 9864/99.

Solution:

Step 1:

Step 2:

Step 3:

Step 4:

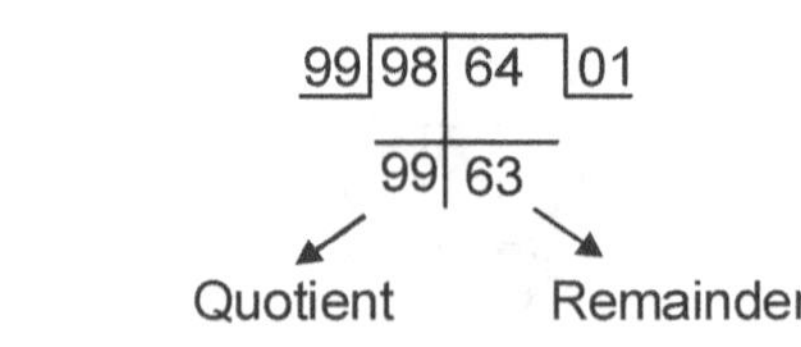

Quotient   Remainder

Example 7.13: 7842/97.

Solution:
Step 1:

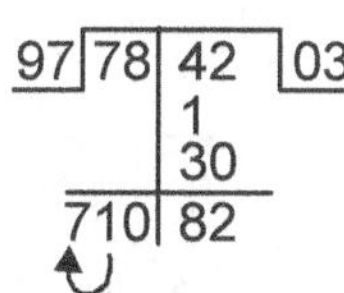

Step 2:

Step 3:

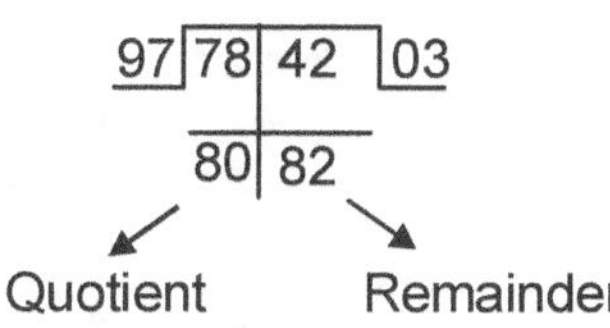

Step 4:

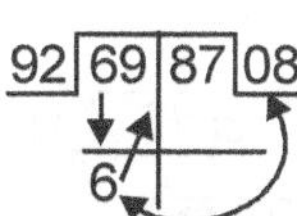

Quotient   Remainder

Example 7.14: 6987/92.

Solution:
Step 1:

Step 2:

Step 3:

Step 4:

Step 5:

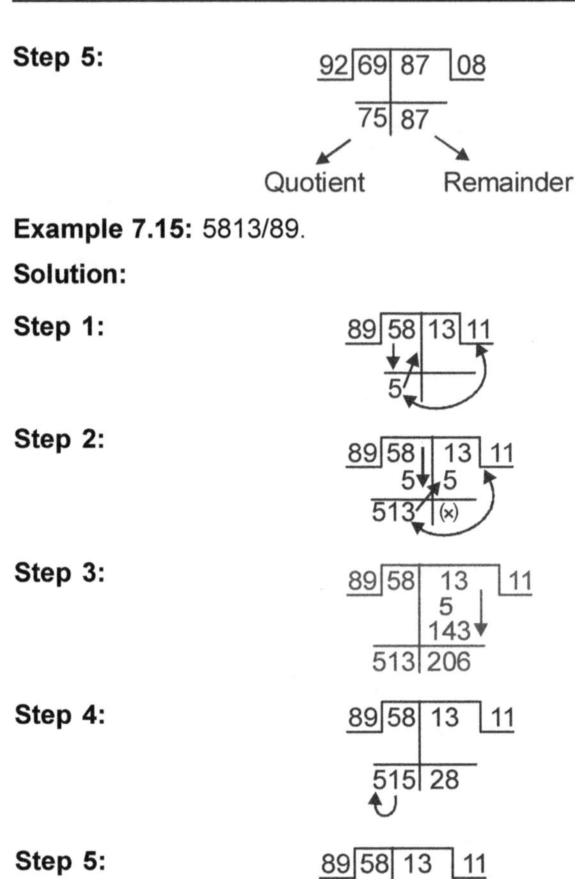

Example 7.15: 5813/89.

Solution:

Step 1:

Step 2:

Step 3:

Step 4:

Step 5:

Exercise for Practice

1.	1254/9	**2.**	2456/8
3.	7643/7	**4.**	7865/5
5.	8923/6	**6.**	9843/99
7.	5643/98	**8.**	6725/95
9.	3267/93	**10.**	9814/91

SQUARE & CUBE ROOTS

Once upon a time there was a man who was very poor but he was a graduate and he applied for the post of a peon in an MNC. His interview went well and he was selected for that post. At the last moment, officials asked him to tell them his E-Mail id. But somehow that person didn't have any email account. So the officials of that company said to him, "Sorry, we cannot give you this job as it is in our policy that every person who is working here should have his email id. The Man became very sad and at that time he was having only ₹500 with him. He decided to make most of it and went directly to the Vegetable Market and bought different vegetables. He went home to home selling those vegetables and somehow till evening he was able to make a profit of ₹300. At that time, he decided to do this business only and as days passed, his business grew and slowly and slowly he bought a shop, then more shops and now he became one of the biggest players in the market of franchise for selling fresh vegetables.

One fine day, a news channel conducted his interview and the reporter asked many questions and at the end he asked him about his email id. On this, the person said, sorry I don't have any email ID. On hearing this, the reporter said, "Are you joking? Don't you know the importance of having an Email id. Don't you know with an Email id you can be an achiever."

The Person replied "Yes an achiever. A peon in an MNC".

Our life is full of opportunities. Somehow we are not able to see them and we curse our destiny that we don't have enough things or opportunities available to us. But somehow we need to understand that whatever opportunities we have with us, we have to make the most out of them and we should have faith in ourselves.

SQUARE ROOTS

Square roots are widely used in Mathematics. But in conventional way, finding square root is a very boring and tedious process. But it is not the case with Vedic, you can find it even without using pen and paper.

Square Root of a Perfect Square:

A Number is a perfect square only when it ends with 0,1,4,5,6 and 9. If a number ends with '0' then it should contain even number of Zeroes.

It is very important to know the last digit of square of various numbers as this method is based on it. Here are the squares and last digit of squares of numbers from 1 - 9.

Numbers	Squares	Last Digit of Squares
1	1	1
2	4	4
3	9	9
4	16	6
5	25	5
6	36	6
7	49	9
8	64	4
9	81	1

It is really interesting to note down that last digit of squares of 2 numbers are same.

Squares	Last Digit
1 and 9	1
2 and 8	4
3 and 7	9
4 and 6	6
5	5

Example 8.1: Find the Square Root of 1296.

Solution:

Step 1: Check whether the digits of number are multiple of 2 or not, if no then simply make it by adding 0 before it.

Divide the given number into 2 boxes by drawing a vertical line. RHB will consist of right most 2 digits and remaining digits will go onto the LHB.

Step 2: Since the last digit of RHB ends with 6, so we have 2 possibilities with us for the last digit of the answer.

$$12\ 96 = \_\,\underline{4}\ \text{or}\ \_\,\underline{6}$$

Step 3: To find the Left digit, find the nearest perfect square below the number present in LHB.

$3^2(9)$ is the nearest perfect square below 12. So we have 34 or 36.

Step 4: Now we have two options with us

$$34\ \text{or}\ 36$$

To know which number is perfect square of 1296, we will calculate the square of 35 as it is the middle term.

$$35^2 = 12\ |\ 25$$

Since $1296 > 1225$

So **36** is the square of **1296.** **Ans.**

Example 8.2: Find the square root of 9801.

Solution:

Step 1: $98\ |\ 01$

Step 2: $98\ |\ 01$

$$\_\,\underline{1}\ \text{or}\ \_\,\underline{9}$$

Step 3: $98\ |\ 01$

$$(9^2)\ 81 < 98$$

$$98 \mid 01 = 91 \text{ or } 99$$

Step 4: $95^2 = 90 \mid 25$

$$9025 < 9801$$

So **99** is the square root of **9801.** **Ans.**

Teacher:	What do you call a person who keeps on talking when people are no longer interested?
Shreya:	A teacher.

Example 8.3: Find the square root of 576.

Solution:

Step 1: $05 \mid 76$

Step 2: $05 \mid 76$

$$\underline{4} \text{ or } \underline{6}$$

Step 3: $05 \mid 76$

$$(2^2) \, 04 < 05$$

$$05 \mid 76 = 24 \text{ or } 26$$

Step 4: $25^2 = 06 \mid 25$

$$0625 > 0576$$

So **24** is the square root of **576.** **Ans.**

Example 8.4: Find the square root of 5329.

Solution:

Step 1: $53 \mid 29$

Step 2: $53 \mid 29$

$$\underline{3} \text{ or } \underline{7}$$

Step 3: $53 \mid 29$

$$(7^2) \, 49 < 53$$

$$53 \mid 29 = 73 \text{ or } 77$$

Step 4 : $\qquad 75^2 = 56 \mid 25$

$$5625 > 5329$$

So **73** is the square root of **5329.** **Ans.**

Example 8.5: Find the square root of 4624.

Solution:

Step 1: $\qquad 46 \mid 24$

Step 2: $\qquad 46 \mid 24$

$$\_\underline{4} \text{ or } \_\underline{6}$$

Step 3: $\qquad 46 \mid 24$

$$(6^2)\ 36 < 46$$

$$46 \mid 24 = 62 \text{ or } 68$$

Step 4: $\qquad 65^2 = 42 \mid 25$

$$4225 < 4624$$

So **68** is the square root of **4624.** **Ans.**

Example 8.6: Find the square root of 3721.

Solution:

Step 1: $\qquad 37 \mid 21$

Step 2: $\qquad 37 \mid 21$

$$\_\underline{1} \text{ or } \_\underline{9}$$

Step 3: $\qquad 37 \mid 21$

$$(6^2)\ 36 < 37$$

$$37 \mid 21 = 61 \text{ or } 69$$

Step 4: $\qquad 65^2 = 42 \mid 25$

$$3721 < 4225$$

So **61** is the square root of **3721.** **Ans.**

Teacher:	Tell the name of Any Microsoft Product?
Sameer:	MS Excel
Riya:	MS Word
Kajal:	MS PowerPoint
Rakesh:	(After Thinking a lot) ...... "MS Dhoni".

Example 8.7: Find the square root of 8464?

Solution:

Step 1:   84 | 64

Step 2:   84 | 64

$$\_\underline{2} \text{ or } \_\underline{8}$$

Step 3:   84 | 64

$$(9^2)\ 81 < 84$$

$$84 \mid 64 = 92 \text{ or } 98$$

Step 4: $95^2 = 90 \mid 25$

$$8464 < 9025$$

So **<u>92</u>** is the square root of **<u>8464.</u>** **Ans.**

Example 8.8: Find the square root of 3025?

Solution:

Step 1:   30 | 25

$$\_\underline{5}$$

Step 3:   30 | 25

$$(5^2)\ 25 < 30$$

$$30 \mid 25 = 55$$

So **<u>55</u>** is the square root of **<u>3025.</u>** **Ans.**

Example 8.9: Find the square root of 1849.

Solution:

Step 1:
$$18 \mid 49$$
$$\_\underline{3} \text{ or } \_\underline{7}$$

Step 3:
$$18 \mid 49$$
$$(4^2)\ 16 < 18$$
$$18 \mid 49 = 43 \text{ or } 47$$

Step 4:
$$45^2 = 20 \mid 25$$
$$1849 < 2025$$

So **43** is the square root of **1849.** **Ans.**

Example 8.10: Find the square root of 7569?

Solution:

Step 1:
$$75 \mid 69$$
$$\_\underline{3} \text{ or } \_\underline{7}$$

Step 2:
$$75 \mid 69$$
$$(8^2)\ 64 < 75$$
$$75 \mid 69 = 83 \text{ or } 87$$

Step 3:
$$85^2 = 72 \mid 25$$
$$7225 < 7569$$

So **87** is the square root of **7569.** **Ans.**

Exercise for Practice

Find the Square root of the following:

1.	1156	**2.**	1521	**3.**	2116
4.	2809	**5.**	3844	**6.**	4624
7.	5041	**8.**	5929	**9.**	6889
10.	8464				

CUBE ROOTS

The process of finding cube root of any number is exactly opposite to that of finding the cube.

Finding the cube root of any given number is very tedious process in conventional way of Mathematics. Rather there might be a possibility that you can commit some errors. But this is not the case with the Vedic way of finding cube root of a number. After some practice you will be able to find it without using pen and paper.

Let us take an example.

If 64 is the cube of 4 then 4 is the cube root of 64.

You can find out the cube roots of perfect cubes by using the similar method which is used to find out the square roots of perfect Squares.

Number	*Cube*	*Last Digit of cube*
1	1	1
2	8	8
3	27	7
4	64	4
5	125	5
6	216	6
7	343	3
8	512	2
9	729	9

Now it is clear that last digit of every number ends with a different number hence making it easy to find the cube root of any perfect cube.

So we can easily conclude from the above that

Last Digit of Cube	*Last Digit of Cube Root*
1	1
8	2

Last Digit of Cube	Last Digit of Cube Root
7	3
4	4
5	5
6	6
3	7
2	8
9	9

Example 8.11: Find the cube root of 39304?

Solution:

Step 1: Firstly, convert the digit of given number into the multiple of 3 like

$$39304 = 039304$$

Step 2: Divide the number equally into 2 boxes (i.e., 3 digits in the LHB and 3 digits in RHB)

$$039 \mid 304$$

Step 3: As number is of 5 or 6 digits, the cube will be of 2 digits.

To find the Right Hand Digit of cube, simply check the corresponding number for 4 from the table.

$$039 \mid 304$$

$$4$$

Step 4: To find the Left Hand Digit of the cube, find the nearest perfect cube below the number present in LHB.

$$039 \mid 304$$

$$27(3^3) < 039 < 64(4^3)$$

Now we have LHB and RHB digit with us which is 34.

Cube root of 39304 is **34. Ans.**

Example 8.12: Find the Cube Root of 328509.

Solution:

Step 1:   328 | 509

Step 2:   Number ends with 9 so the RHB digit is 9

Step 3:   Nearest Perfect Cube below the number present in LHB is

328 | 509

$216(6^3) < 328 < 343(7^3)$

Now we have both the digits with us which is 69

Cube Root of 328509 is <u>69.</u> **Ans.**

Example 8.13: Find the Cube Root of 68921.

Solution:

Step 1:   68 | 921

Step 2:   Number ends with 1 so the RHB digit is 1

Step 3:   Nearest Perfect Cube below the number present in LHB is

68 | 921

$64(4^3) < 68 < 125(5^3)$

Now we have both the digits with us which is 41

Cube Root of 68921 is <u>41.</u> **Ans.**

A **donkey** kicked Shyam and ran away, Shyam **ran** to catch the donkey.

He saw a **zebra** and started beating it and said, '**Acha tracksuit pahan ke dhoka de raha hai**'.

Example 8.14: Find the Cube Root of 148877.

Solution:

Step 1:   148 | 877

Step 2:   Number ends with 7 so the RHB digit is 3

Step 3:   Nearest Perfect Cube below the number present in LHB is

148 | 877

$$125(5^3) < 148 < 216(6^3)$$

Now we have both the digits with us which is 53

Cube Root of 148877 is **53.** **Ans.**

Example 8.15: Find the Cube Root of 24389.

Solution:

Step 1:   24 | 389

Step 2:   Number ends with 9 so the RHB digit is 9

Step 3:   Nearest Perfect Cube below the number present in LHB is

24 | 389

$$8(2^3) < 24 < 27(3^3)$$

Now we have both the digits with us which is 29

Cube Root of 24389 is **29.** **Ans.**

Example 8.16: Find the Cube Root of 373248.

Solution:

Step 1:   373 | 248

Step 2:   Number ends with 8 so the RHB digit is 2

Step 3:   Nearest Perfect Cube below the number present in LHB is

373 | 248

$$343(7^3) < 373 < 512(8^3)$$

Now we have both the digits with us which is 72

Cube Root of 373248 is **72.** **Ans.**

Teacher:	Manas, Why are you doing your math multiplication on the floor?
Manas:	You told me to do it without using tables.

Example 8.17: Find the Cube Root of 614125.

Solution:

Step 1:   614 | 125

Step 2:   Number ends with 5 so the RHB digit is 5

Step 3:   Nearest Perfect Cube below the number present in LHB is

$$614 \mid 125$$

$512(8^3) < 614 < 729(9^3)$

Now we have both the digits with us which is 85

Cube Root of 614125 is **85. Ans.**

Example 8.18: Find the Cube Root of 830584.

Solution:

Step 1:   830 | 584

Step 2:   Number ends with 4 so the RHB digit is 4

Step 3:   Nearest Perfect Cube below the number present in LHB is

$$830 \mid 584$$

$729(9^3) < 830 < 1000(10^3)$

Now we have both the digits with us which is 94

Cube Root of 830584 is **94. Ans.**

Example 8.19: Find the Cube Root of 884736.

Solution:

Step 1:   884 | 736

Step 2:   Number ends with 6 so the RHB digit is 6

Step 3:   Nearest Perfect Cube below the number present in LHB is

$$884 \mid 736$$

$729(9^3) < 884 < 1000(10^3)$

Now we have both the digits with us which is 96

Cube Root of 884736 is **96. Ans.**

Example 8.20: Find the Cube Root of 970299.

Solution:

Step 1:   970 | 299

Step 2:   Number ends with 9 so the RHB digit is 9

Step 3: Nearest Perfect Cube below the number present in LHB is

970 | 299

$729(9^3) < 970 < 1000(10^3)$

Now we have both the digits with us which is 99

Cube Root of 970299 is **99.** **Ans.**

Exercise for Practice

Find the Cube root of the following questions:

11.	12167	**12.**	21952
13.	35937	**14.**	68921
15.	103823	**16.**	166375
17.	238328	**18.**	405224
19.	636056	**20.**	753571

OUT OF BOX METHODS

As a man walked on a desolate beach, he began to see another figure, far in the distance. Slowly, the two approached each other and he could make out a local native who kept leaning down, picking something up and throwing it out into the water. Time and again, he hurled things into the ocean.

As the distance between them continued to narrow, the man could see that the native was picking up starfish that had been washed upon the beach and, one at a time, was throwing them back into the water. Puzzled, the man approached the native and asked what he was doing. "I'm throwing these starfish back into the ocean. You see, it's low tide right now and all of these starfish have been washed up onto the shore. If I don't throw them back into the sea, they'll die here from lack of oxygen."

"But there must be thousands of starfish on this beach," the man replied. "You can't possibly get to all of them. There are just too many. And this same thing is probably happening on hundreds of beaches all up and down this coast. Can't you see that you can't possibly make a difference?"

The local native smiled, bent down and picked up another starfish, and as he threw it back into the sea he replied, "Made a difference to that one!"

MULTIPLYING A NUMBER WITH SERIES OF NINE

Example 9.1: Multiply 24 × 99.

Solution:

Step 1:   Write down both the numbers one above the other as shown below

$$
\begin{array}{c|c}
2 \quad 4 & \\
9 \quad 9 & \\
\hline
\text{LHB} & \text{RHB}
\end{array}
$$

Step 2:   To calculate the value of LHB, simply calculate the difference between 99 and the nearest base, i.e., 100 to give 01(100 − 99) and subtract the difference from the number.

$$\text{LHB} = 24 - 01 = 23$$

Step 3:   Now to calculate the value of RHB, subtract the number, i.e., 24 from the above used base.

$$\text{RHB} = 100 - 24 = 76$$

$$
\begin{array}{c|c}
2 \quad 4 & \\
9 \quad 9 & \\
\hline
23 & 76
\end{array}
$$

$$= 2376 \text{ **Ans.**}$$

> **Note:** *RHB will always contain the same number of digits as the number of zeros in the nearest base of the given number.*

Example 9.2: Multiply 67 × 99.

Solution:

Step 1:

$$
\begin{array}{c|c}
6 \quad 7 & \\
9 \quad 9 & \\
\hline
\text{LHB} & \text{RHB}
\end{array}
$$

Step 2: $\text{LHB} = 67 - 1 = 66$

Step 3: $\text{RHB} = 100 - 67 = 33$

$$\begin{array}{c|c} 6 \quad 7 \\ 9 \quad 9 \\ \hline 66 & 33 \end{array}$$

= 6633 **Ans.**

Mother:	How come you never bring any books home?
Daughter:	Mummy, they're schoolbooks, not home books.

Example 9.3: Multiply 739 × 999.

Solution:

Step 1: Write down both the numbers one above the other as shown below

$$\begin{array}{c|c} 7 \quad 3 \quad 9 \\ 9 \quad 9 \quad 9 \\ \hline LHB & RHB \end{array}$$

Step 2: To calculate the value of LHB, simply calculate the difference between 999 and the nearest base, i.e., 1000 to give 01(1000 − 999) and subtract the difference from the number.

$$LHB = 739 - 01 = 738$$

Step 3: Now to calculate the value of RHB, subtract the number, i.e., 739 from the above used base.

$$RHB = 1000 - 739 = 261$$

$$\begin{array}{c|c} 7 \quad 3 \quad 9 \\ 9 \quad 9 \quad 9 \\ \hline 738 & 261 \end{array}$$

= 738261 **Ans.**

> **Note:** *RHB will always contain the same number of digits as the number of zeros in the nearest base of the given number.*

Example 9.4: Multiply 834 × 999.

Solution:

Step 1:

```
 8   3   4
 9   9   9
─────────────
 LHB  │  RHB
```

Step 2:   LHB = 834 − 1 = 833

Step 3:   RHB = 1000 − 834 = 166

```
 8   3   4
 9   9   9
─────────────
 833  │  166
```

= 833166 **Ans.**

Father:	How did your exams go?
Son:	I got nearly 100 in every subject.
Father:	What do you mean, nearly 100?
Son:	I was just a digit out; I averaged 10!

Example 9.5: Multiply 8167 × 9999.

Solution:

Step 1:   Write down both the numbers one above the other as shown below

```
 8   1   6   7
 9   9   9   9
─────────────────
  LHB   │  RHB
```

Step 2:   To calculate the value of LHB, simply calculate the difference between 9999 and the nearest base, i.e., 10000 to give 01(10000 − 9999) and subtract the difference from the number.

LHB = 8167 − 01 = 8166

Step 3:   Now to calculate the value of RHB, subtract the number, i.e., 8167 from the above used base.

RHB = 10000 − 8167 = 1833

$$
\begin{array}{cccc}
8 & 1 & 6 & 7 \\
9 & 9 & 9 & 9 \\
\hline
\end{array}
$$

$$8166 \mid 1833$$

$$= 81661833 \textbf{ Ans.}$$

> **Note:** *RHB will always contain the same number of digits as the number of zeros in the nearest base of the given number.*

Example 9.6: Multiply 3265 × 9999.

Solution:

Step 1:

$$
\begin{array}{cccc}
3 & 2 & 6 & 5 \\
9 & 9 & 9 & 9 \\
\hline
\end{array}
$$

$$\text{LHB} \mid \text{RHB}$$

Step 2: LHB = 3265 – 1 = 3264

Step 3: RHB = 10000 – 3265 = 6735

$$
\begin{array}{cccc}
3 & 2 & 6 & 5 \\
9 & 9 & 9 & 9 \\
\hline
\end{array}
$$

$$3264 \mid 6735$$

$$= 32646735 \textbf{ Ans.}$$

Example 9.7: Multiply 98 × 999.

Solution:

Step 1: Write down both the numbers one above the other as shown below. Convert the 2 digit number to 3 digits by adding a 0 from left most side.

$$
\begin{array}{ccc}
0 & 9 & 8 \\
9 & 9 & 9 \\
\hline
\end{array}
$$

$$\text{LHB} \mid \text{RHB}$$

Step 2: To calculate the value of LHB, simply calculate the difference between 999 and the nearest base, i.e., 1000 to give 01(1000 – 999) and subtract the difference from the number.

$$\text{LHB} = 98 – 01 = 97$$

Step 3: Now to calculate the value of RHB, subtract the number, i.e., 098 from the above used base.

$$RHB = 1000 - 098 = 901$$

$$
\begin{array}{ccc}
0 & 9 & 8 \\
9 & 9 & 9 \\
\hline
97 & | & 901
\end{array}
$$

$$= 97901 \textbf{ Ans.}$$

> **Note:** *RHB will always contain the same number of digits as the number of zeros in the nearest base of the given number.*

Example 9.8: Multiply 763 × 9999.

Solution:

Step 1:

$$
\begin{array}{cccc}
0 & 7 & 6 & 3 \\
9 & 9 & 9 & 9 \\
\hline
\text{LHB} & | & \text{RHB}
\end{array}
$$

Step 2: LHB = 763 − 1 = 762

Step 3: RHB = 10000 − 763 = 9237

$$
\begin{array}{cccc}
0 & 7 & 6 & 3 \\
9 & 9 & 9 & 9 \\
\hline
762 & | & 9237
\end{array}
$$

$$= 7629237 \textbf{ Ans.}$$

Example 9.9: Multiply 321 × 9999.

Solution:

Step 1:

$$
\begin{array}{cccc}
0 & 3 & 2 & 1 \\
9 & 9 & 9 & 9 \\
\hline
\text{LHB} & | & \text{RHB}
\end{array}
$$

Step 2: LHB = 321 − 1 = 320

Step 3: RHB = 10000 − 321 = 9679

$$= 3209679 \textbf{ Ans.}$$

Example 9.10: Multiply 892 × 9999.

Solution:

Step 1:

0 8 9 2

9 9 9 9

LHB | RHB

Step 2:   LHB = 892 − 1 = 891

Step 3:   RHB = 10000 − 892 = 9108

= 8919108 **Ans.**

Exercise for Practice

Solve the following questions:

1.	75 × 99	**2.**	78 × 99
3.	832 × 999	**4.**	984 × 999
5.	43 × 999	**6.**	67 × 999
7.	7643 × 9999	**8.**	8954 × 9999
9.	785 × 9999	**10.**	324 × 9999

MULTIPLYING A NUMBER WITH SERIES OF 1

Example 9.11: Multiply 35 × 11.

Solution:

Step 1: Write down both the numbers one above the other as shown below.

$$
\begin{array}{cc}
3 & 5 \\
1 & 1 \\
\hline
\text{III} \mid \text{II} \mid \text{I}
\end{array}
$$

> **Note:** *The number of boxes will be 1 less than the number of digits in the question.*

Step 2: In box I, Right most digit of number, i.e., 5 of 35 will come.

$$
\begin{array}{cc}
3 & 5 \\
1 & 1 \\
\hline
\text{III} \mid \text{II} \mid 5
\end{array}
$$

Step 3: In box III, left most digit of number, i.e., 3 of 35 will come.

$$
\begin{array}{cc}
3 & 5 \\
1 & 1 \\
\hline
3 \mid \text{II} \mid 5
\end{array}
$$

Step 4: In box II, add value of both the boxes, i.e., 5 + 3 = 8.

$$
\begin{array}{cc}
3 & 5 \\
1 & 1 \\
\hline
3 \mid 8 \mid 5
\end{array}
$$

= 385 **Ans.**

Example 9.12: Multiply 67 × 11.

Solution:

Step 1:

$$
\begin{array}{cc}
6 & 7 \\
1 & 1 \\
\hline
\text{III} \mid \text{II} \mid \text{I}
\end{array}
$$

Step 2:

$$\begin{array}{cc} 6 & 7 \\ 1 & 1 \\ \hline \text{III} \mid \text{II} \mid 7 \end{array}$$

Step 3:

$$\begin{array}{cc} 6 & 7 \\ 1 & 1 \\ \hline 6 \mid \text{II} \mid 7 \end{array}$$

Step 4:

$$\begin{array}{cc} 6 & 7 \\ 1 & 1 \\ \hline 6 \mid 13 \mid 7 \end{array}$$

(By using the concept of carryover)

$$7 \mid 3 \mid 7$$

= 737 **Ans.**

Example 9.13: Multiply 436 × 11.

Solution:

Step 1: Write down both the numbers one above the other as shown below.

$$\begin{array}{ccc} 4 & 3 & 6 \\ & 1 & 1 \\ \hline \text{IV} \mid \text{III} \mid \text{II} \mid \text{I} \end{array}$$

> **Note:** *The number of boxes will be 1 less than the number of digits in the question.*

Step 2: In box I, of number, i.e., 6 of 436 will come.

$$\begin{array}{ccc} 4 & 3 & 6 \\ & 1 & 1 \\ \hline \text{IV} \mid \text{III} \mid \text{II} \mid 6 \end{array}$$

Step 3: In box IV, right most digit of number, i.e., 4 of 436 will come.

$$\begin{array}{ccc} 4 & 3 & 6 \\ & 1 & 1 \\ \hline 4 \mid \text{III} \mid \text{II} \mid 6 \end{array}$$

Step 4: In box II, add the value of right 2 digits of the number 436, i.e., 3 + 6 = 9.

4   3   6

1   1

---

4 | III | 9 | 6

Step 5: In box III, add the value of left 2 digit numbers, i.e., 4 + 3 = 7

4   3   6

1   1

---

4 | 7 | 9 | 6

= 4796 **Ans.**

Example 9.14: Multiply 612 × 11.

Solution:

Step 1:

6   1   2

1   1

IV | III | II | I

Step 2:

6   1   2

1   1

IV | III | II | 2

Step 3:

6   1   2

1   1

---

6 | III | II | 2

Step 4:

6   1   2

1   1

---

6 | III | 3 | 2

Step 5:

6   1   2

1   1

---

6 | 7 | 3 | 2

= 6732 **Ans.**

Example 9.15: Multiply 254 × 111.

Solution:

Step 1: Write down both the numbers one above the other as shown below.

$$
\begin{array}{ccc}
2 & 5 & 4 \\
1 & 1 & 1 \\
\hline
\end{array}
$$

V	IV	III	II	I

> **Note:** *The number of boxes will be 1 less than the number of digits in the question.*

Step 2: In box I, Right most digit of number, i.e., 4 of 254 will come.

$$
\begin{array}{ccc}
2 & 5 & 4 \\
1 & 1 & 1 \\
\hline
\end{array}
$$

V	IV	III	II	4

Step 3: In box V, right most digit of number, i.e., 2 of 254 will come.

$$
\begin{array}{ccc}
2 & 5 & 4 \\
1 & 1 & 1 \\
\hline
\end{array}
$$

V	IV	III	II	4

Step 4: In box II, add the 2 rightmost digits of the number, i.e., 5 + 4 = 9.

$$
\begin{array}{ccc}
2 & 5 & 4 \\
1 & 1 & 1 \\
\hline
\end{array}
$$

2	IV	III	9	4

Step 5: In box III, add all the 3 digits of the number, i.e., 2 + 5 + 4 = 11

$$
\begin{array}{ccc}
2 & 5 & 4 \\
1 & 1 & 1 \\
\hline
\end{array}
$$

2	IV	11	9	4

Step 6: In box IV, add the 2 leftmost digits of the number, i.e., 2 + 5 = 7

$$\begin{array}{cccc} 2 & 5 & 4 \\ 1 & 1 & 1 \end{array}$$

$$2 \mid 7 \mid 11 \mid 9 \mid 4$$

$$2 \mid 7 \mid \mathbf{11} \mid 9 \mid 4$$

$$2\ 8\ 1\ 9\ 4$$

$$= 28194 \textbf{ Ans.}$$

Example 9.16: Multiply 321 × 111.

Solution:

Step 1:

$$\begin{array}{ccc} 3 & 2 & 1 \\ 1 & 1 & 1 \end{array}$$

$$V \mid IV \mid III \mid II \mid I$$

Step 2:

$$\begin{array}{ccc} 3 & 2 & 1 \\ 1 & 1 & 1 \end{array}$$

$$V \mid IV \mid III \mid II \mid 1$$

Step 3:

$$\begin{array}{ccc} 3 & 2 & 1 \\ 1 & 1 & 1 \end{array}$$

$$3 \mid IV \mid III \mid II \mid 1$$

Step 4:

$$\begin{array}{ccc} 3 & 2 & 1 \\ 1 & 1 & 1 \end{array}$$

$$2 \mid IV \mid III \mid 3 \mid 1$$

Step 5:

$$\begin{array}{ccc} 3 & 2 & 1 \\ 1 & 1 & 1 \end{array}$$

$$3 \mid IV \mid 6 \mid 3 \mid 1$$

Step 6:

$$\begin{array}{ccc} 3 & 2 & 1 \\ 1 & 1 & 1 \end{array}$$

$$3 \mid 5 \mid 6 \mid 3 \mid 1$$

$$= 35631 \textbf{ Ans.}$$

Example 9.17: Multiply 5402 × 1111.

Solution:

Step 1: Write down both the numbers one above the other as shown below.

5 4 0 2

1 1 1 1

VII | VI | V | IV | III | II | I

> **Note:** *The number of boxes will be 1 less than the number of digits in the question.*

Step 2: In box I, Right most digit of number, i.e., 2 of 5402 will come.

5 4 0 2

1 1 1 1

VII | VI | V | IV | III | II | 2

Step 3: In box VII, Left most digit of number, i.e., 5 of 5402 will come.

5 4 0 2

1 1 1 1

5 | VI | V | IV | III | II | 2

Step 4: In box II, add the 2 rightmost digits of the number, i.e., 0 + 2 = 2.

5 4 0 2

1 1 1 1

5 | VI | V | IV | III | 2 | 2

Step 5: In box III, add the 3 rightmost digits of the number, i.e., 4 + 0 + 2 = 6

5 4 0 2

1 1 1 1

5 | VI | V | IV | 6 | 2 | 2

Step 6: In box IV, add all the 4 digits of the number, i.e., $5 + 4 + 0 + 2 = 11$

	5	4	0	2			
		1	1	1	1		
5	VI	V	11	6	2	2	

Step 7: In box V, add the 3 leftmost digits of the number, i.e., $5 + 4 + 0 = 9$

	5	4	0	2			
		1	1	1	1		
5	VI	9	11	6	2	2	

Step 8: In box VI, add the 2 leftmost digits of the number, i.e., $5 + 4 = 9$.

	5	4	0	2			
		1	1	1	1		
5	9	9	11	6	2	2	

5 | 9 | 9 | 11 | 6 | 2 | 2

= 6001622 **Ans.**

Father:	Why did you get such a low score in that test?
Son:	Absence.
Father:	You were absent on the day of the test?
Son:	No, but the boy who sits next to me was!

Exercise for Practice

Solve the following questions:

11. 93×11 **12.** 87×11

13. 53×11 **14.** 654×111

15. 873×111 **16.** 521×111

UNFORGETTABLE DATES AND CALENDAR

> *Imagine there is a bank, which credits your account each morning with ₹ 86,400, carries over no balance from day to day, allows you to keep no cash balance, and every evening cancels whatever part of the amount you had failed to use during the day. What would you do? Draw out every penny, of course!*
>
> *Well, everyone has such a bank. Its name is Time.*
>
> *Every morning, it credits you with 86,400 seconds. Every night it writes off, as lost, whatever of this you have failed to invest for good purpose. It carries over no balance. It allows no overdraft. Each day it opens a new account for you. Each night it burns the records of the day. If you fail to use the day's deposits, the loss is yours.*
>
> *There is no going back. There is no drawing against the "tomorrow."*
>
> *Therefore, there is never not enough time or too much time. Time management can be only done by us. It is never the case of us not having enough time to do things, but the case of whether we want to do things or not.*

Managing time in this world full of competition is very difficult. But the person who knows the art of time management can touch the sky. No doubt that's why in various competitive exams questions on Dates and Calendar are asked regularly.

Remembering dates is really a tedious work to do. But with the help of below discussed techniques it willl be a game full of fun.

Let us the understand some of the terms which are used in the given chapter.

Extra Days: In a given period, the number of days which are more than the complete weeks are called Extra Days.

For Example: Find out the total number of Extra Days in 265 days.

Solution: First of all we have to find complete number of weeks in 265 days

$$265 = (259 + 6) \text{ days}$$

$$265 = 37 \text{ weeks} + 6 \text{ days}$$

Now these 6 days are called Extra Days.

For every Century (100 years) there are specified numbers of Extra Days which are given below

Years	Extra Days
100	5
200	3
300	1
400	0
500	5
600	3
700	1
800	0
900	5
1000	3
1100	1
1200	0
1300	5
1400	3

Years	Extra Days
1500	1
1600	0
1700	5
1800	3
1900	1
2000	0

It is clear that Extra days are repeating after 400 years.

This can be shown below the help of a table:

Years	Extra Days
100, 500, 900, 1300, 1700	5
200, 600, 1000, 1400, 1800	3
300, 700, 1100, 1500, 1900	1
400, 800, 1200, 1600, 2000	0

Similary, we can say

1 Normal Year = 365 days = 52 × 7 + 1 = 1 Extra Day

1 Leap Year = 366 days = 52 × 7 + 2 = 2 Extra Days

Note: *Every 4th year between 1-99 years is Leap Year.*

We have also allotted a particular number (0-6) to each day of the week which is given below:

Days	Sunday	Monday	Tuesday	Wednesday	Thursday	Friday	Saturday
Number	0	1	2	3	4	5	6

By using all the above information, let us understand the concept with the help of the following question.

Example 10.1: Which day of the week was on 5th Jan. 1998?

Solution: To know the day, we have to find out the Extra Number of days in the above date.

Let us first find out Extra days in year, i.e., we have to find till 1997.

$$1997 = 1900 + 97$$

We know

In 1900 years, there is 1 Extra Day.

In 97 Years, there are 24 Leap Years and 73 Normal Years.

Therefore,

$$97 \text{ Years} = 24 \times 2 + 73 \times 1$$
$$= 48 + 73$$
$$= 121$$
$$= 119 + 2$$
$$= 0 + 2$$
$$97 \text{ Years} = 2 \text{ Extra Days.}$$

Now let us find out Extra days in Month.

$$5^{th} \text{ January} = 5 \text{ Extra Days}$$

In 5th January 1998 = (5 + 2 + 1) Extra Days = 1 Extra Day.

So, it is clear that on 5th January 1998, the day was Monday.

Example 10.2: Which day of the week was on 10th March 2012?

Solution: To know the day, we have to find out the Extra Number of days in the above date.

Let us first find out Extra days in year, i.e., we have to find till 2012.

$$2012 = 2000 + 11$$

We know

In 2000 years, there is 0 Extra Day.

In 11 Years, there are 2 Leap Years and 9 Normal Years.

Therefore,

$$12 \text{ Years} = 2 \times 2 + 9 \times 1$$
$$= 4 + 9 = 13 = 7 + 6 = 6$$
$$12 \text{ Years} = 6 \text{ Extra Days.}$$

Now let us find out Extra days in Month.

January	February	March
31 days	29 days	10
3 Extra Days	1 Extra Days	3 Extra Days

10th March = 7 or 0 Extra Days.

In 10th March 2012 = (0 + 6 + 0) Extra Days = 6 Extra Day.

So, it is clear that on 10th March 2012, the day was Saturday.

Example 10.3: On what dates of April 2002 did Sunday fall?

Solution: Let us find the day on 1.4.2002

2002 has 2 Extra Days.

Now let us find out Extra days in Month

January	February	March	April
3 ED	0 ED	3 ED	0 ED

31st March = 6 Extra Days

In 31st March 2002 = (2 + 6) Extra Days = 8 or 1 Extra Day.

So, 1st April 2002 was Monday.

So on 7th, 14th, 21st and 28th it was Sunday.

Example 10.4: On what dates of June 1902 did Tuesday fall?

Solution: Let us find the day on 1.6.1900

1902 has 3 Extra Days.

Now let us find out Extra days in Month

January	February	March	April	May	June
3 ED	0 ED	3 ED	2ED	3ED	0ED

Till 31st May = 11 Extra Days.

Upto 31st May 1902   = (3 + 11) Extra Days

                      = 14 or 0 Extra Days.

So, 1st June 1902 was Monday.

So on 3rd, 10th, 17th and 24th it was Tuesday.

Exercise for Practice

Solve the following questions:

1. Which day of the week was on 10th June 1996?
2. Which day of the week was on 15th April 1992?
3. Which day of the week was on 3rd May 1900?
4. On what dates of August 1983 did Saturday fall?
5. On what dates of December 2008 did Monday fall?

TIPS FOR COMPETITIVE EXAMS

"Recipe for Success: Study while others are sleeping; work while others are loafing; prepare while others are playing; and dream while others are wishing."   **—By William A Ward**

Life is not a bed of roses. And this starts from the very beginning of our life. When we start our school life, we start facing exams. In this era of cut throat competition, excelling in exams is of utmost importance. One can excel in exam through practice. As the famous saying goes "Practice makes a man perfect", so for scoring good marks you have to practice a lot. As an exam is not only about attempting questions and writing answers, it is also a test of one's patience. No doubt most of us do a lot of hard work but how many of us prepare according to the exam! Understanding the pattern, keeping the required speed, being accurate are all important factors to nail an exam.

Try to give mock papers of the exam you are going to appear for, be it for Engineering, Medical, Armed Forces, MBA, CA, Jobs in Government as well as Private Sector, every where you will realize the magic of practice. Plus, try to measure the improvement in speed and accuracy with every paper that you give. Time Management is yet another important thing which distinguishes between winners and losers. Many students finish the test on time but there is no time left for filling the OMR. Many a times even after solving the paper correctly, some students commit errors while filling the answers on the OMR sheet. So, please keep track of time. Just remember this line said by Robert Collier "Success is the sum of small efforts, repeated day in and day out".

GENERAL & LINEAR EQUATIONS

Till now we have discussed about the use of Vedic Mathematics in arithmetic part of Mathematics. Let us discuss some techniques for algebra part also as it is also equally important.

The traditional way of solving equations is not encouraging for students as there is no creativity about it. But with the help of certain formulae of Vedic Mathematics anyone can solve equations mentally.

Let us understand the concept by solving this simple equation.

$$mx + a = nx + b$$

By using Vedic Mathematics, we can directly calculate the value of x by using the given formula which is

$$x = b - a / m - n$$

For Example:

Example 12.1: Solve for x

$$5x + 1 = x + 9$$

Solution: We know

$$mx + a = nx + b$$

$$x = (b - a) / (m - n)$$

By comparing we can find

$m = 5$, $a = 1$, $n = 1$ and $b = 9$

So, $\qquad\qquad x = 9 - 1 / 5 - 1$

$$x = 8/4 = 2$$

Thus $\qquad x = 2$ **Ans.**

Example 12.2: Solve for x

$$9x + 21 = 6x + 42$$

Solution: We know

$$mx + a = nx + b$$

$$x = (b - a) / (m - n)$$

By comparing we can find

$m = 9$, $a = 21$, $n = 6$ and $b = 42$

So, $\qquad x = 42 - 21 / 9 - 6$

$$x = 21/3 = 7$$

Thus $\qquad x = 7$ **Ans.**

For solving General Equations of degree two, we have to use the following procedure.

Let the equation be

$$(x + m) (x + n) = (x + a) (x + b)$$

Then the value of x can be calculated as

$$x = ab - mn / (m + n) - (a + b)$$

Example 12.3: Solve for x

$$(x + 2) (x + 4) = (x + 3) (x + 6)$$

Solution: We know

$$(x + m) (x + n) = (x + a) (x + b)$$

$$x = ab - mn / (m + n) - (a + b)$$

By comparing we can find

$m = 2$, $n = 4$, $a = 3$ and $b = 6$

So, $\qquad x = 3 \times 6 - 2 \times 7/(2 + 4) - (3 + 6)$

$$x = 18 - 8/6 - 9$$

$$x = -10/3 \text{ \textbf{Ans.}}$$

Example 12.4: Solve for x

$$(x + 9)(x + 6) = (x - 3)(x - 6)$$

Solution: We know

$$(x + m)(x + n) = (x + a)(x + b)$$

$$x = ab - mn / (m + n) - (a + b)$$

By comparing we can find

$m = 9$, $n = 6$, $a = -3$ and $b = -6$

So,

$$x = (-3) \times (-6) - 9 \times 6/(9 + 6) - \{(-3) + (-6)\}$$

$$x = 18 - 54/15 + 9$$

$$x = -36/24 = -3/2 \textbf{ Ans.}$$

Exercise for Practice

Solve the following questions for *x*:

1. $x + 8 = x + 6$
2. $x + 3 = x - 7$
3. $x + 5 = x + 3$
4. $x + 6 = x - 4$
5. $(x + 2)(x + 6) = (x + 8)(x + 5)$
6. $(x + 5)(x + 7) = (x - 6)(x - 1)$

SIMULTANEOUS LINEAR EQUATIONS

These are the type of equations in which 2 variables are present along with a constant. We cannot calculate the value of the variables by using a single equation. For calculating the values of both the variables, we need 2 equations. Linear Equation with 2 variables are shown below:

$$ax + by = c$$

$$mx + ny = p$$

Now with the use of Vedic Mathematics, we have derived a direct formula for finding the value of x and y.

For x:

$$x = (bp - nc) / (mb - an)$$
$$y = (mc - ap) / (mb - an)$$

Let us understand this concept by solving the Questions.

Example 12.5: Solve for x and y.

$$5x + 2y = 8$$
$$3x + 4y = 6$$

Solution: We know

$$ax + by = c$$
$$mx + ny = p$$

By comparing, we have

$a = 5$, $b = 2$, $c = 8$, $m = 3$, $n = 4$, $p = 6$.

For finding the value of x and y, we have direct formula

$$x = (bp - nc) / (mb - an)$$
$$x = (2 \times 6 - 4 \times 8) / (3 \times 2 - 5 \times 4)$$
$$x = (12 - 32) / (6 - 20)$$
$$x = -20 / -14 = 10/7$$
$$y = (mc - ap) / (mb - an)$$
$$y = (3 \times 8 - 5 \times 6) / (3 \times 2 - 5 \times 4)$$
$$y = (24 - 30) / (6 - 20)$$
$$y = -6 / -14 = 3/7$$

Thus, $x = 10/7$ and $y = 3/7$ **Ans.**

Example 12.6: Solve for x and y.

$$8x + 5y = 6$$
$$4x + 2y = 4$$

Solution: We know

$$ax + by = c$$
$$mx + ny = p$$

By comparing, we have

$a = 8$, $b = 5$, $c = 6$, $m = 4$, $n = 2$, $p = 4$.

For finding the value of x and y, we have direct formula

$$x = (bp - nc) / (mb - an)$$
$$x = (5 \times 4 - 2 \times 6) / (4 \times 5 - 8 \times 2)$$
$$x = (20 - 12) / (20 - 16)$$
$$x = 8 / 4 = 2$$
$$y = (mc - ap) / (mb - an)$$
$$y = (4 \times 6 - 8 \times 4) / (4 \times 5 - 8 \times 2)$$
$$y = (24 - 32) / (20 - 16)$$
$$y = -8 / 4 = -2$$

Thus, $x = 2$ and $y = -2$ **Ans.**

Exercise for Practice

Solve the following questions for x and y:

7. $3x + 4y = 8$

   $5x + 7y = 9$

8. $9x + 5y = 7$

   $7x + 6y = 8$

9. $6x + 8y = 2$

   $3x + 7y = 5$

10. $x + 7y = 9$

    $4x + 6y = 7$

TEST PAPERS FOR PRACTICE

"Practice does not make perfect. Only perfect practice makes perfect."

—Vince Lombardi

Test Paper–I

Time taken : .....

Solve the following questions by applying techniques of Vedic mathematics which you have learned by this book.

1.	98 × 1 0 2 Ans:	**2.**	1 9 3 × 9 9 9 Ans:	**3.**	1 2 1 3 × 7 6 3 Ans:
4.	7 4 × 1 1 Ans:	**5.**	1 8 2 4 × 3 2 1 8 Ans:	**6.**	98^2 Ans:
7.	31^2 Ans:	**8.**	24^3 Ans:	**9.**	81^3 Ans:
10.	$(1369)^{1/2}$ Ans:	**11.**	$(5041)^{1/2}$ Ans:	**12.**	$(226981)^{1/3}$ Ans:
13.	$(54872)^{1/3}$ Ans:	**14.**	981/6 Ans:	**15.**	6972/9 Ans:

Test Paper–2

Time taken : .....

Solve the following questions by applying techniques of Vedic mathematics which you have learned by this book.

1.
$$74 \times 86$$
Ans:

2.
$$109 \times 106$$
Ans:

3.
$$789 \times 999$$
Ans:

4.
$$158 \times 621$$
Ans:

5.
$$6981 \times 4210$$
Ans:

6. 73^2

Ans:

7. 99^2

Ans:

8. 42^3

Ans:

9. 51^3

Ans:

10. $(2704)^{1/2}$

Ans:

11. $(3969)^{1/2}$

Ans:

12. $(357911)^{1/3}$

Ans:

13. $(274625)^{1/3}$

Ans:

14. $1024/5$

Ans:

15. $912/6$

Ans:

Test Paper–3

Time taken : .....

Solve the following questions by applying techniques of Vedic mathematics which you have learned by this book.

1.
$$\begin{array}{r} 9\ 8 \\ \times\ 1\ 1 \\ \hline \end{array}$$
Ans:

2.
$$\begin{array}{r} 6\ 7 \\ \times\ 8\ 1 \\ \hline \end{array}$$
Ans:

3.
$$\begin{array}{r} 4\ 9 \\ \times\ 9\ 9 \\ \hline \end{array}$$
Ans:

4.
$$\begin{array}{r} 7\ 8\ 6 \\ \times\ 4\ 2\ 1 \\ \hline \end{array}$$
Ans:

5.
$$\begin{array}{r} 9\ 1\ 2 \\ \times\ 1\ 0\ 4\ 6 \\ \hline \end{array}$$
Ans:

6. 42^2

Ans:

7. 86^2

Ans:

8. 91^3

Ans:

9. 63^3

Ans:

10. $(2916)^{1/2}$

Ans:

11. $(4225)^{1/2}$

Ans:

12. $(5832)^{1/3}$

Ans:

13. $(328509)^{1/3}$

Ans:

14. $5961/8$

Ans:

15. $9816/7$

Ans:

Test Paper–4

Time taken : .....

Solve the following questions by applying techniques of Vedic mathematics which you have learned by this book.

1.　　　　　69
　　　　　× 9 9
　　　　　————
Ans:

2.　　　　　7 2
　　　　　× 8 7
　　　　　————
Ans:

3.　　　　　7 6 9
　　　　　× 1 0 3
　　　　　————
Ans:

4.　　　　　1 0 8
　　　　　× 1 1 0
　　　　　————
Ans:

5.　　　　　9 1 2 3
　　　　　× 1 4 2 1
　　　　　————
Ans:

6. 39^2
Ans:

7. 64^2
Ans:

8. 31^3
Ans:

9. 62^3
Ans:

10. $(8649)^{1/2}$
Ans:

11. $(3721)^{1/2}$
Ans:

12. $(132651)^{1/3}$
Ans:

13. $(238328)^{1/3}$
Ans:

14. 1582/7
Ans:

15. 1942/8
Ans:

Test Paper–5

Time taken : .....

Solve the following questions by applying techniques of Vedic mathematics which you have learned by this book.

1.
$$\begin{array}{r} 95 \\ \times\ 73 \\ \hline \end{array}$$
Ans:

2.
$$\begin{array}{r} 121 \\ \times\ 539 \\ \hline \end{array}$$
Ans:

3.
$$\begin{array}{r} 129 \\ \times\ 661 \\ \hline \end{array}$$
Ans:

4.
$$\begin{array}{r} 59 \\ \times\ 99 \\ \hline \end{array}$$
Ans:

5.
$$\begin{array}{r} 7250 \\ \times\ 4195 \\ \hline \end{array}$$
Ans:

6. 81^2

Ans:

7. 36^2

Ans:

8. 13^3

Ans:

9. 45^3

Ans:

10. $(3025)^{1/2}$

Ans:

11. $(4489)^{1/2}$

Ans:

12. $(287496)^{1/3}$

Ans:

13. $(91125)^{1/3}$

Ans:

14. $4985/99$

Ans:

15. $8321/98$

Ans:

Test Paper–6

Time taken : .....

Solve the following questions by applying techniques of Vedic mathematics which you have learned by this book.

1.
$$113 \times 108$$
Ans:

2.
$$2158 \times 9999$$
Ans:

3.
$$168 \times 365$$
Ans:

4.
$$747 \times 111$$
Ans:

5.
$$48246 \times 22183$$
Ans:

6. 48^2

Ans:

7. 52^2

Ans:

8. 28^3

Ans:

9. 91^3

Ans:

10. $(1849)^{1/2}$

Ans:

11. $(7569)^{1/2}$

Ans:

12. $(250047)^{1/3}$

Ans:

13. $(531441)^{1/3}$

Ans:

14. $7684/97$

Ans:

15. $5432/96$

Ans:

Test Paper–7

Time taken : .....

Solve the following questions by applying techniques of Vedic mathematics which you have learned by this book.

1.   9 6 4
    × 1 3 2

Ans:

2.   6 8 4
    × 9 9 9

Ans:

3.   3 2 1 3
    × 7 6 3 7

Ans:

4.   7 4 5
    × 1 1 1

Ans:

5.   5 8 3 4 2
    × 2 8 1 8 7

Ans:

6. 91^2

Ans:

7. 28^2

Ans:

8. 22^3

Ans:

9. 71^3

Ans:

10. $(1369)^{1/2}$

Ans:

11. $(8281)^{1/2}$

Ans:

12. $(778688)^{1/3}$

Ans:

13. $(117649)^{1/3}$

Ans:

14. 7388/95

Ans:

15. 3643/99

Ans:

Test Paper–8

Time taken : .....

Solve the following questions by applying techniques of Vedic mathematics which you have learned by this book.

1.
$$\begin{array}{r} 9\ 8\ 3 \\ \times\ 1\ 1\ 1 \\ \hline \end{array}$$
Ans:

2.
$$\begin{array}{r} 4\ 9\ 1\ 3 \\ \times\ 9\ 9\ 9\ 9 \\ \hline \end{array}$$
Ans:

3.
$$\begin{array}{r} 1\ 2\ 1 \\ \times\ 1\ 0\ 5 \\ \hline \end{array}$$
Ans:

4.
$$\begin{array}{r} 6\ 7\ 3 \\ \times\ 3\ 2\ 7 \\ \hline \end{array}$$
Ans:

5.
$$\begin{array}{r} 6\ 7\ 2\ 3\ 9 \\ \times\ 3\ 2\ 7\ 6\ 4 \\ \hline \end{array}$$
Ans:

6. 72^2
Ans:

7. 88^2
Ans:

8. 74^3
Ans:

9. 45^3
Ans:

10. $(7744)^{1/2}$
Ans:

11. $(1024)^{1/2}$
Ans:

12. $(804357)^{1/3}$
Ans:

13. $(42875)^{1/3}$
Ans:

14. 453/6
Ans:

15. 7894/98
Ans:

Test Paper–9

Time taken : .....

Solve the following questions by applying techniques of Vedic mathematics which you have learned by this book.

1.
     2 4 7
   × 1 8 2

Ans:

2.
    6 3 2 8
   × 9 9 9 9

Ans:

3.
    2 1 6 7
   × 8 6 4

Ans:

4.
      8 4
   × 1 0 1

Ans:

5.
   1 3 9 7 6
 × 3 8 9 2 1

Ans:

6. 22^2

Ans:

7. 44^2

Ans:

8. 68^3

Ans:

9. 46^3

Ans:

10. $(1681)^{1/2}$

Ans:

11. $(9025)^{1/2}$

Ans:

12. $(804357)^{1/3}$

Ans:

13. $(42875)^{1/3}$

Ans:

14. $6542/7$

Ans:

15. $7645/9$

Ans:

Test Paper–10

Time taken : .....

Solve the following questions by applying techniques of Vedic mathematics which you have learned by this book.

1.
$$\begin{array}{r} 89 \\ \times\,1\,1\,2 \\ \hline \end{array}$$
Ans:

2.
$$\begin{array}{r} 4\,3\,7 \\ \times\,9\,9\,9 \\ \hline \end{array}$$
Ans:

3.
$$\begin{array}{r} 1\,9\,3\,3 \\ \times\,8\,5\,3\,8 \\ \hline \end{array}$$
Ans:

4.
$$\begin{array}{r} 9\,4\,3 \\ \times\,1\,1\,1 \\ \hline \end{array}$$
Ans:

5.
$$\begin{array}{r} 7\,7\,9\,4\,3 \\ \times\,8\,6\,8\,2\,7 \\ \hline \end{array}$$
Ans:

6. 85^2

Ans:

7. 69^2

Ans:

8. 93^3

Ans:

9. 61^3

Ans:

10. $(9604)^{1/2}$

Ans:

11. $(7225)^{1/2}$

Ans:

12. $(636056)^{1/3}$

Ans:

13. $(778688)^{1/3}$

Ans:

14. $5327/96$

Ans:

15. $7643/99$

Ans:

SOLUTIONS

EFFORTLESS MULTIPLICATION

Q.1. 111 × 113.

Solution:

```
1 1 1    +11
1 1 3    +13
─────────────
 124  | +143
```

= 12543 **Ans.**

Q.2. 108 × 114.

Solution:

```
1 0 8    +08
1 1 4    +14
─────────────
 122  | +112
```

= 12312 **Ans.**

Q.3. 106 × 116.

Solution:

```
1 0 6    +06
1 1 6    +16
─────────────
 122  | +96
```

= 12296 **Ans.**

Q.4. 101 × 117.

Solution:

$$
\begin{array}{r|l}
1\ 0\ 1 & +01 \\
1\ 1\ 7 & +17 \\
\hline
118 & +17 \\
\end{array}
$$

= 11817 **Ans.**

Q.5. 103 × 109.

Solution:

$$
\begin{array}{r|l}
1\ 0\ 3 & +03 \\
1\ 0\ 9 & +09 \\
\hline
112 & +27 \\
\end{array}
$$

= 11227 **Ans.**

Q.6. 1012 × 1009.

Solution:

$$
\begin{array}{r|l}
1\ 0\ 1\ 2 & +012 \\
1\ 0\ 0\ 9 & +009 \\
\hline
1021 & +108 \\
\end{array}
$$

= 1021108 **Ans.**

Q.7. 1005 × 1011.

Solution:

$$
\begin{array}{r|l}
1\ 0\ 0\ 5 & +005 \\
1\ 0\ 1\ 1 & +011 \\
\hline
1016 & +055 \\
\end{array}
$$

= 1016055 **Ans.**

Q.8. 1003 × 1016

Solution:

$$
\begin{array}{r|l}
1\ 0\ 0\ 3 & +003 \\
1\ 0\ 1\ 6 & +016 \\
\hline
1019 & +048 \\
\end{array}
$$

= 1019048 **Ans.**

Q.9. 1008 × 1001.

Solution:

$$
\begin{array}{rl}
1\ 0\ 0\ 8 & +008 \\
1\ 0\ 0\ 1 & +001 \\
\hline
1009 \mid & +008 \\
\end{array}
$$

= 1009008 **Ans.**

Q.10. 1017 × 1006.

Solution:

$$
\begin{array}{rl}
1\ 0\ 1\ 7 & +017 \\
1\ 0\ 0\ 6 & +006 \\
\hline
1023 \mid & +102 \\
\end{array}
$$

= 1023102 **Ans.**

Q.11. 89 × 98.

Solution:

$$
\begin{array}{rl}
8\ 9 & -11 \\
9\ 8 & -02 \\
\hline
87 \mid & +22 \\
\end{array}
$$

= 8722 **Ans.**

Q.12. 85 × 97.

Solution:

$$
\begin{array}{rl}
8\ 5 & -15 \\
9\ 7 & -03 \\
\hline
82 \mid & +45 \\
\end{array}
$$

= 8245 **Ans.**

Q.13. 91 × 96.

Solution:

$$
\begin{array}{rl}
9\ 1 & -09 \\
9\ 6 & -04 \\
\hline
87 \mid & +36 \\
\end{array}
$$

= 8736 **Ans.**

Q.14. 93 × 95.

Solution:

$$
\begin{array}{c|c}
9\ 3 & -07 \\
9\ 5 & -05 \\
\hline
88 & +35
\end{array}
$$

= 8835 **Ans.**

Q.15. 97 × 92.

Solution:

$$
\begin{array}{c|c}
9\ 7 & -03 \\
9\ 2 & -08 \\
\hline
89 & +24
\end{array}
$$

= 8924 **Ans.**

Q.16. 99 × 88.

Solution:

$$
\begin{array}{c|c}
9\ 9 & -01 \\
8\ 8 & -12 \\
\hline
87 & +12
\end{array}
$$

= 8712 **Ans.**

Q.17. 988 × 999.

Solution:

$$
\begin{array}{c|c}
9\ 8\ 8 & -012 \\
9\ 9\ 9 & -001 \\
\hline
987 & +012
\end{array}
$$

= 987012 **Ans.**

Q.18. 986 × 992.

Solution:

$$
\begin{array}{c|c}
9\ 8\ 6 & -014 \\
9\ 9\ 2 & -008 \\
\hline
978 & +112
\end{array}
$$

= 978112 **Ans.**

Q.19. 996 × 985.

Solution:

```
9 9 6    –004
9 8 5    –015
─────────────
  981  | +060
```

= 981060 **Ans.**

Q.20. 997 × 990.

Solution:

```
9 9 7    –003
9 9 0    –010
─────────────
  987  | +030
```

= 987030 **Ans.**

Q.21 106 × 98.

Solution:

```
1 0 6    +06
  9 8    –02
─────────────
  104  | –12
```

= 10388 **Ans.**

Q.22. 101 × 96

Solution:

```
1 0 1    +01
  9 6    –04
─────────────
   97  | –04
```

= 9696 **Ans.**

Q.23. 103 × 95.

Solution:

```
1 0 3    +03
  9 5    –05
─────────────
   98  | –15
```

= 9785 **Ans.**

Q.24. 107 × 92.

Solution:

$$
\begin{array}{r|l}
1\ 0\ 7 & +07 \\
9\ 2 & -08 \\
\hline
99 & -56 \\
\end{array}
$$

= 9844 **Ans.**

Q.25. 109 × 88.

Solution:

$$
\begin{array}{r|l}
1\ 0\ 9 & +09 \\
8\ 8 & -12 \\
\hline
97 & -108 \\
\end{array}
$$

= 9592 **Ans.**

Q.26. 1008 × 999.

Solution:

$$
\begin{array}{r|l}
1\ 0\ 0\ 8 & +008 \\
9\ 9\ 9 & -001 \\
\hline
1007 & -008 \\
\end{array}
$$

= 1006992 **Ans.**

Q.27. 1014 × 992.

Solution:

$$
\begin{array}{r|l}
1\ 0\ 1\ 4 & +014 \\
9\ 9\ 2 & -008 \\
\hline
1006 & -112 \\
\end{array}
$$

= 1005888 **Ans.**

Q.28. 1019 × 985.

Solution:

$$
\begin{array}{r|l}
1\ 0\ 1\ 9 & +019 \\
9\ 8\ 5 & -015 \\
\hline
1004 & -285 \\
\end{array}
$$

= 1003715 **Ans.**

Q.29. 1015 × 990.

Solution:

$$
\begin{array}{r|l}
1\ 0\ 1\ 5 & +015 \\
9\ 9\ 0 & -010 \\
\hline
1005 & -150
\end{array}
$$

= 1004850 **Ans.**

Q.30. 1011 × 993.

Solution:

$$
\begin{array}{r|l}
1\ 0\ 1\ 1 & +011 \\
9\ 9\ 3 & -007 \\
\hline
1004 & -077
\end{array}
$$

= 1003923 **Ans.**

Q.31. 69 × 53.

Solution:

$$
\begin{array}{c}
6\quad 9 \\
5\quad 3 \\
\hline
30\ \mid\ 63\ \mid\ 27
\end{array}
$$

= 3657 **Ans.**

Q.32. 77 × 81.

Solution:

$$
\begin{array}{c}
7\quad 7 \\
8\quad 1 \\
\hline
56\ \mid\ 63\ \mid\ 7
\end{array}
$$

= 6237 **Ans.**

Q.33. 78 × 82.

Solution:

$$
\begin{array}{c}
7\quad 8 \\
8\quad 2 \\
\hline
56\ \mid\ 78\ \mid\ 16
\end{array}
$$

= 6396 **Ans.**

Q.34. 55 × 62.

Solution:

$$
\begin{array}{ccc}
5 & 5 \\
6 & 2 \\
\hline
30 \mid 40 \mid 10
\end{array}
$$

= 3410 **Ans.**

Q.35. 99 × 67.

Solution:

$$
\begin{array}{ccc}
9 & 9 \\
6 & 7 \\
\hline
54 \mid 117 \mid 63
\end{array}
$$

= 6633 **Ans.**

Q.36. 98 × 32.

Solution:

$$
\begin{array}{ccc}
9 & 8 \\
3 & 2 \\
\hline
27 \mid 42 \mid 16
\end{array}
$$

= 3136 **Ans.**

Q.37. 234 × 765.

Solution:

$$
\begin{array}{cccc}
2 & 3 & 4 \\
7 & 6 & 5 \\
\hline
14 \mid 33 \mid 56 \mid 39 \mid 20
\end{array}
$$

= 179010 **Ans.**

Q.38. 987 × 126.

Solution:

$$
\begin{array}{cccc}
9 & 8 & 7 \\
1 & 2 & 6 \\
\hline
9 \mid 26 \mid 77 \mid 62 \mid 42
\end{array}
$$

= 124362 **Ans.**

Q.39. 911 × 348.

Solution:

	9	1	1	
	3	4	8	
27	39	79	12	8

= 317028 **Ans.**

Q.40. 881 × 467.

Solution:

	8	8	1	
	4	6	7	
32	80	108	62	7

= 411427 **Ans.**

Q.41. 653 × 421.

Solution:

	6	5	3	
	4	2	1	
24	32	28	11	3

= 274913 **Ans.**

Q.42. 786 × 654.

Solution:

	7	8	6	
	6	5	4	
42	83	104	62	24

= 514044 **Ans.**

Q.43. 999 × 24.

Solution:

	9	9	9	
	0	2	4	
0	18	54	54	36

= 23976 **Ans.**

Q.44. 987 × 43.

Solution:

```
        9   8   7
        0   4   3
    ─────────────────
    0 │ 36 │ 59 │ 52 │ 21
```

= 42441 **Ans.**

Q.45. 678 × 43.

Solution:

```
        6   7   8
        0   4   3
    ─────────────────
    0 │ 24 │ 46 │ 53 │ 24
```

= 29154 **Ans.**

Q.46. 762 × 87.

Solution:

```
        7   6   2
        0   8   7
    ─────────────────
    0 │ 56 │ 97 │ 58 │ 14
```

= 66294 **Ans.**

Q.47. 1236 × 9873.

Solution:

```
      1   2   3   6
      9   8   7   3
  ──────────────────────────
  9 │ 26 │ 50 │ 95 │ 75 │ 51 │ 18
```

= 12203028 **Ans.**

Q.48. 9836 × 4376.

Solution:

```
      9   8   3   6
      4   3   7   6
  ──────────────────────────────
  36 │ 59 │ 99 │ 143 │ 87 │ 60 │ 36
```

= 43042336 **Ans.**

Q.49. 7623 × 2765.

Solution:

```
          7   6   2   3
          2   7   6   5
      ─────────────────────────────
      14 | 61 | 88 | 91 | 63 | 28 | 15
```

= 21077595 **Ans.**

Q.50. 1289 × 5342.

Solution:

```
          1   2   8   9
          5   3   4   2
      ─────────────────────────────
      5 | 13 | 50 | 79 | 63 | 52 | 18
```

= 6885838 **Ans.**

Q.51. 9832 × 675.

Solution:

```
          9   8   3   2
          0   6   7   5
      ─────────────────────────────
      0 | 54 | 111 | 119 | 73 | 29 | 10
```

= 6636600 **Ans.**

Q.52. 1239 × 234.

Solution:

```
          1   2   3   9
          0   2   3   4
      ─────────────────────────────
      0 | 2 | 7 | 16 | 35 | 39 | 36
```

= 289926 **Ans.**

Q.53. 4674 × 875.

Solution:

```
          4   6   7   4
          0   8   7   5
      ─────────────────────────────
      0 | 32 | 76 | 118 | 111 | 63 | 20
```

= 4089750 **Ans.**

Q.54. 7324 × 876.

Solution:

		7	3	2	4
	0	8	7	6	

0	56	73	79	64	40	24

= 6415824 **Ans.**

Q.55. 78541 × 34252.

Solution:

	7	8	5	4	1
3	4	2	5	2	

21	52	61	83	83	53	32	13	2

= 2690186332 **Ans.**

Q.56. 95432 × 98656.

Solution:

9	5	4	3	2
9	8	6	5	6

81	117	130	134	145	84	51	28	12

= 9414939392 **Ans.**

Q.57. 87543 × 89643.

Solution:

8	7	5	4	3
8	9	6	4	3

64	128	151	151	142	92	49	24	9

= 7847617149 **Ans.**

Q.58. 87564 × 23548.

Solution:

8	7	5	6	4
2	3	5	4	8

16	38	71	94	143	118	84	64	32

= 2061957072 **Ans.**

MAGICAL SQUARES

Q.1. 35^2.

Solution:

$= 3 \times 4 \mid 5^2$

$= 1225$ **Ans.**

Q.2. 45^2.

Solution:

$= 4 \times 5 \mid 5^2$

$= 2025$ **Ans.**

Q.3. 55^2.

Solution:

$= 5 \times 6 \mid 5^2$

$= 3025$ **Ans.**

Q.4. 65^2.

Solution:

$= 6 \times 7 \mid 5^2$

$= 4225$ **Ans.**

Q.5. 75^2.

Solution:

$= 7 \times 8 \mid 5^2$

$= 5625$ **Ans.**

Q.6. 105^2.

Solution:

$= 10 \times 11 \mid 5^2$

$= 11025$ **Ans.**

Q.7. 115^2.

Solution:

$= 11 \times 12 \mid 5^2$

$= 13225$ **Ans.**

Q.8. 135^2.

Solution:

$= 13 \times 14 \mid 5^2$

$= 18225$ **Ans.**

Q.9. 145^2.

Solution:

$= 14 \times 15 \mid 5^2$

$= 21025$ **Ans.**

Q.10. 155^2.

Solution: $= 15 \times 16 \mid 5^2$

                      $= 24025$ **Ans.**

Q.11. 79^2.

Solution: $= 79 - 21 \mid 441$

                      $= 6241$ **Ans.**

Q.12. 86^2.

Solution: $= 86 - 14 \mid 196$

                      $= 7396$ **Ans.**

Q.13. 89^2.

Solution: $= 89 - 11 \mid 121$

                      $= 7921$ **Ans.**

Q.14. 92^2.

Solution: $= 92 - 08 \mid 64$

                      $= 8464$ **Ans.**

Q.15. 94^2.

Solution: $= 94 - 06 \mid 36$

                      $= 8836$ **Ans.**

Q.16. 106^2.

Solution: $= 106 + 06 \mid 36$

                      $= 11236$ **Ans.**

Q.17. 109^2.

Solution: $= 109 + 09 \mid 81$

                      $= 11881$ **Ans.**

Q.18. 111^2.

Solution: $= 111 + 11 \mid 121$

                      $= 12321$ **Ans.**

Q.19. 114^2.

Solution: = 114 + 14 | 196

                             = 12996 **Ans.**

Q.20. 119^2.

Solution: = 119 + 19 | 361

                             = 14161 **Ans.**

Q.21. 53^2.

Solution: = 25 | 30 | 9

                             = 2809 **Ans.**

Q.22. 45^2.

Solution: = 16 | 40 | 25

                             = 2025 **Ans.**

Q.23. 67^2.

Solution: = 36 | 84 | 49

                             = 4489 **Ans.**

Q.24. 89^2.

Solution: = 64 | 144 | 81

                             = 7921 **Ans.**

Q.25. 91^2.

Solution: = 81 | 18 | 01

                             = 8281 **Ans.**

Q.26. 81^2.

Solution: = 64 | 16 | 01

                             = 6561 **Ans.**

Q.27. 87^2.

Solution: = 64 | 112 | 49

                             = 7569 **Ans.**

Q.28. 32^2.

Solution: = 09 | 12 | 04

= 1024 **Ans.**

Q.29. 97^2.

Solution: = 81 | 126 | 49

= 9409 **Ans.**

Q.30. 64^2.

Solution: = 36 | 48 | 16

= 4096 **Ans.**

Q.31. 153^2.

Solution: = 1 | 10 | 31 | 30 | 9

= 23409 **Ans.**

Q.32. 245^2.

Solution: = 4 | 16 | 36 | 40 | 25

= 60025 **Ans.**

Q.33. 671^2.

Solution: = 36 | 84 | 61 | 14 | 1

= 450241 **Ans.**

Q.34. 909^2.

Solution: = 81 | 0 | 162 | 0 | 81

= 826281 **Ans.**

Q.35. 191^2.

Solution: = 1 | 18 | 83 | 18 | 1

= 36481 **Ans.**

Q.36. 581^2.

Solution: = 25 | 80 | 74 | 16 | 1

= 337561 **Ans.**

Q.37. 807^2.

Solution: = 64 | 0 | 112 | 0 | 49

= 651249 **Ans.**

Q.38. 325^2.

Solution: = 9 | 12 | 34 | 20 | 25

= 105625 **Ans.**

Q.39. 812^2.

Solution: = 64 | 16 | 33 | 4 | 4

= 659344 **Ans.**

Q.40. 923^2.

Solution: = 81 | 36 | 58 | 12 | 9

= 851929 **Ans.**

PAINLESS CUBES

Q.1. 23^3.

Solution: = 8 | 36 | 54 | 27

= 12167 **Ans.**

Q.2. 55^3.

Solution: = 125 | 375 | 375 | 125

= 166375 **Ans.**

Q.3. 37^3.

Solution: = 27 | 189 | 441 | 343

= 50653 **Ans.**

Q.4. 89^3.

Solution: = 512 | 1728 | 1944 | 729

= 704969 **Ans.**

Q.5. 41^3.

Solution: = 64 | 48 | 12 | 1

= 68921 **Ans.**

Q.6. 71^3.

Solution: $= 343 \mid 147 \mid 21 \mid 1$

$= 357911$ **Ans.**

Q.7. 27^3.

Solution: $= 8 \mid 84 \mid 294 \mid 343$

$= 19683$ **Ans.**

Q.8. 52^3.

Solution: $= 125 \mid 150 \mid 60 \mid 8$

$= 140608$ **Ans.**

Q.9. 99^3.

Solution: $= 729 \mid 2187 \mid 2187 \mid 729$

$= 970299$ **Ans.**

Q.10. 76^3.

Solution: $= 343 \mid 882 \mid 756 \mid 216$

$= 438976$ **Ans.**

FRIENDLY DIVISION

Q.1. $1254 \div 9$.

Solution: =

$$9 \overline{)\ 12 \mid 54 \mid 1}$$
$$\overline{139 \mid 3}$$

Quotient   Remainder

Q.2. $2456 \div 8$.

Solution: =

$$8 \overline{)\ 24 \mid 56 \mid 2}$$
$$\overline{307 \mid 0}$$

Quotient   Remainder

Q.3. 7643 ÷ 7.

Solution: =

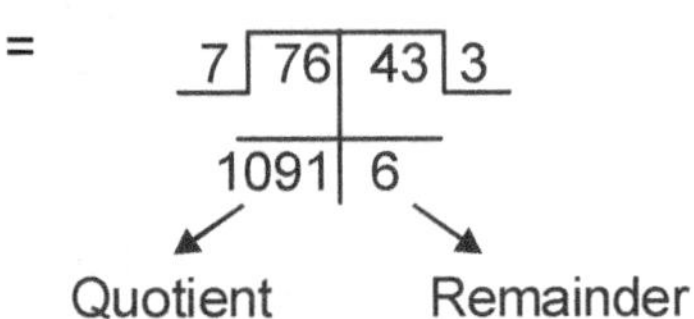

Q.4. 7865 ÷ 5.

Solution: =

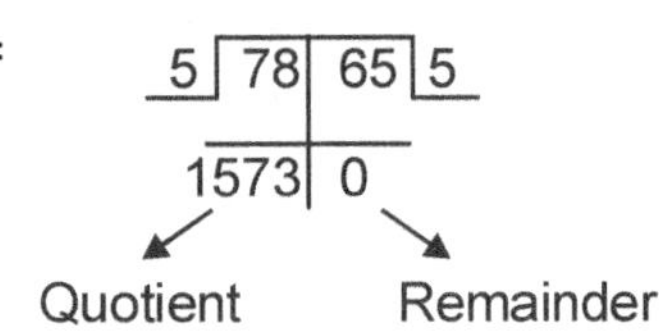

Q.5. 8923 ÷ 6.

Solution: =

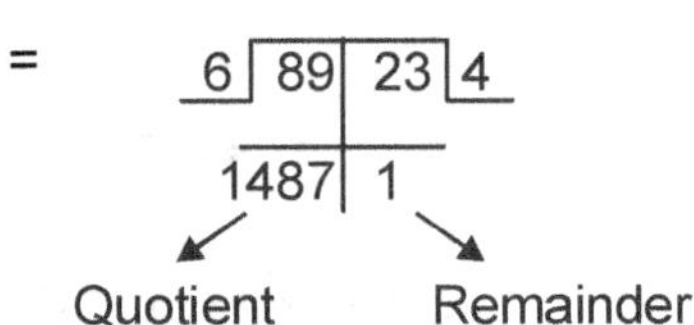

Q.6. 9843 ÷ 99.

Solution: =

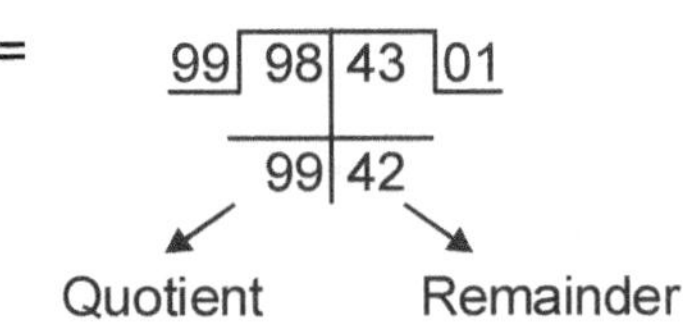

Q.7. 5643 ÷ 98.

Solution: =

Q.8. 6725 ÷ 95.

Solution:　　　　　=

Q.9. 3267 ÷ 93.

Solution:　　　　　=

Q.10. 9814 ÷ 91.

Solution:　　　　　=

SQUARE AND CUBE ROOTS

Q.1. $(1156)^{1/2}$.

Solution:　　　　　$= 34$ or 36

$$35^2 = 1225$$

Since 1156 is smaller than 1225

$$(1156)^{1/2} = 34 \textbf{ Ans.}$$

Q.2. $(1521)^{1/2}$.

Solution:　　　　　$= 31$ or 39

$$35^2 = 1225$$

Since 1521 is greater than 1225

$$(1521)^{1/2} = 39 \textbf{ Ans.}$$

Q.3. $(2116)^{1/2}$.

Solution:
$$= 44 \text{ or } 46$$
$$45^2 = 2025$$

Since 2116 is greater than 2025
$$(2116)^{1/2} = 46 \textbf{ Ans.}$$

Q.4. $(2809)^{1/2}$.

Solution:
$$= 53 \text{ or } 57$$
$$55^2 = 3025$$

Since 2809 is smaller than 3025
$$(2809)^{1/2} = 53 \textbf{ Ans.}$$

Q.5. $(3844)^{1/2}$.

Solution:
$$= 62 \text{ or } 68$$
$$65^2 = 4225$$

Since 3844 is smaller than 4225
$$(3844)^{1/2} = 62 \textbf{ Ans.}$$

Q.6. $(4624)^{1/2}$.

Solution:
$$= 62 \text{ or } 68$$
$$65^2 = 4225$$

Since 4624 is greater than 4225
$$(4624)^{1/2} = 68 \textbf{ Ans.}$$

Q.7. $(5041)^{1/2}$.

Solution:
$$= 71 \text{ or } 79$$
$$75^2 = 5625$$

Since 5041 is smaller than 5625
$$(5041)^{1/2} = 71 \textbf{ Ans.}$$

Q.8. $(5929)^{1/2}$.

Solution:
$$= 73 \text{ or } 77$$
$$75^2 = 5625$$

Since 5929 is greater than 5625

$(5929)^{1/2}$ = 77 **Ans.**

Q.9. $(6889)^{1/2}$.

Solution: = 83 or 87

85^2 = 7225

Since 6889 is greater than 7225

$(6889)^{1/2}$ = 83 **Ans.**

Q.10. $(8464)^{1/2}$.

Solution: = 92 or 98

95^2 = 9025

Since 8464 is smaller than 9025

$(8464)^{1/2}$ = 92 **Ans.**

Q.11. $(12167)^{1/3}$.

Solution: LHB = 2

RHB = 3

= 23 **Ans.**

Q.12. $(21952)^{1/3}$.

Solution: LHB = 2

RHB = 8

= 28 **Ans.**

Q.13. $(35937)^{1/3}$.

Solution: LHB = 3

RHB = 3

= 33 **Ans.**

Q.14. $(68921)^{1/3}$.

Solution: LHB = 4

RHB = 1

= 41 **Ans.**

Q.15. (103823)$^{1/3}$.

Solution: LHB = 4

                                 RHB = 7

                                 = 47 **Ans.**

Q.16. (166375)$^{1/3}$.

Solution: LHB = 5

                                 RHB = 5

                                 = 55 **Ans.**

Q.17. (238328)$^{1/3}$.

Solution: LHB = 6

                                 RHB = 2

                                 = 62 **Ans.**

Q.18. (405224)$^{1/3}$.

Solution: LHB = 7

                                 RHB = 4

                                 = 74 **Ans.**

Q.19. (636056)$^{1/3}$.

Solution: LHB = 8

                                 RHB = 6

                                 = 86 **Ans.**

Q.20. (753571)$^{1/3}$.

Solution: LHB = 9

                                 RHB = 1

                                 = 91 **Ans.**

OUT OF BOX METHODS

Q.1. 75 × 99.

Solution: LHB = 74

                                 RHB = 25

                                 = 7425 **Ans.**

Q.2. 78 × 99.

Solution:

LHB = 77

RHB = 22

= 7722 **Ans.**

Q.3. 832 × 999.

Solution:

LHB = 831

RHB = 168

= 831168 **Ans.**

Q.4. 984 × 999.

Solution:

LHB = 983

RHB = 016

= 983016 **Ans.**

Q.5. 43 × 999

Solution:

LHB = 42

RHB = 957

= 42957 **Ans.**

Q.6. 67 × 999.

Solution:

LHB = 66

RHB = 933

= 66933 **Ans.**

Q.7. 7643 × 9999.

Solution:

LHB = 7642

RHB = 2357

= 76422357 **Ans.**

Q.8. 8954 × 9999.

Solution:

LHB = 8953

RHB = 1046

= 89531046 **Ans.**

Q.9. 785 × 9999.

Solution: LHB = 784

RHB = 9215

= 7849215 **Ans.**

Q.10. 324 × 9999.

Solution: LHB = 323

RHB = 9676

= 3239676 **Ans.**

Q.11. 93 × 11.

Solution: I = 3

II = 12

III = 9

= 429 **Ans.**

Q.12. 87 × 11

Solution: I = 7

II = 15

III = 8

= 957 **Ans**

Q.13. 53 × 11.

Solution: I = 3

II = 8

III = 5

= 583 **Ans.**

Q.14. 654 × 111.

Solution: I = 4

II = 9

III = 15

IV = 11

V = 6

= 72594 **Ans.**

Q.15. 873 × 111.

Solution:

$$\text{I} = 3$$
$$\text{II} = 10$$
$$\text{III} = 18$$
$$\text{IV} = 15$$
$$\text{V} = 8$$
$$= 96903 \textbf{ Ans.}$$

Q.16. 521 × 111.

Solution:

$$\text{I} = 1$$
$$\text{II} = 3$$
$$\text{III} = 8$$
$$\text{IV} = 7$$
$$\text{V} = 5$$
$$= 57831 \textbf{ Ans.}$$

UNFORGETTABLE DATES AND CALENDAR

Q.1. Which day of the week was on 10th June 1996?

Solution:

$$1995 = (1900 + 95) \text{ Years}$$
$$1995 = 0 \text{ Extra Day}$$

Up to 10th June = 1 Extra Day

So, up to 10th June 1996 there is 1 Extra Day.

So, it was Monday.

Q.2. Which day of the week was on 15th April 1992?

Solution:

$$1991 = (1900 + 91) \text{ Years}$$
$$1991 = 2 \text{ Extra Days}$$

Up to 15th April = 1 Extra Day

So, up to 15th April 1992 there is 3 Extra Days.

So it was Wednesday.

Q.3. Which day of the week was on 3rd May 1900?

Solution: 1900 = 0 Extra Day

Up to 3rd May = 4 Extra Days

So, up to 3rd May 1900 there is 4 Extra Days.

So, it was Friday.

Q.4. On what dates of August 1983 did Saturday fall?

Solution: 1982 = 5 Extra Days

Up to 31st July = 2 Extra Days

So, up to 31st July 1983 there is 7 Extra Days.

So, 1st August was Monday. On 6th, 13th, 20th and 27th August it was Saturday.

Q.5. On what dates of December 2008 did Monday fall?

Solution: 2007 = 1 Extra Day

Up to 31st November = 6 Extra Days

So, up to 31st November 2008 there is 7 Extra Days.

So, 1st December was Monday. On 1st, 8th, 15th, 22nd and 29th December it was Monday.

GENERAL & LINEAR EQUATIONS

Q.1. $x + 8 = x + 6$.

Solution: $x = -6 - 8/6 - 4$

$x = -14/2 = -7$ **Ans.**

Q.2. $x + 3 = x - 7$.

Solution: $x = -7 - 3/3 - 9$

$x = -10/-6 = 5/3$ **Ans.**

Q.3. $x + 5 = x + 3$.

Solution: $x = 3 - 5/8 - 7$

$x = -2/1 = -2$ **Ans.**

Q.4. $x + 6 = x - 4$.

Solution: $x = -4 - 6/6 - 3$

$x = -10/3$ **Ans.**

Q.5. $(x + 2)(x + 6) = (x + 8)(x + 5)$.

Solution:　　　　　　　　$x = 40 - 12/8 - 13$

　　　　　　　　　　　　$x = -28/5$ **Ans.**

Q.6. $(x + 5)(x + 7) = (x - 6)(x - 1)$.

Solution:　　　　　　　　$x = 6 - 35/12 - 6$

　　　　　　　　　　　　$x = -29/6$ **Ans.**

Q.7. $3x + 4y = 8$

　　　$5x + 7y = 9$

Solution:　　　　　　　　$x = 36 - 56/20 - 21 = 20$

　　　　　　　　　　　　$y = 40 - 27/20 - 21 = -13$

　　　$x = 20$ and $y = -13$ **Ans.**

Q.8. $9x + 5y = 7$

　　　$7x + 6y = 8$

Solution:　　　　　　　　$x = 40 - 42/35 - 54 = 2/19$

　　　　　　　　　　　　$y = 49 - 72/35 - 54 = 23/19$

　　　$x = 2/19$ and $y = 23/19$ **Ans.**

Q.9. $6x + 8y = 2$

　　　$3x + 7y = 5$

Solution:　　　　　　　　$x = 40 - 14/24 - 42 = -13/9$

　　　　　　　　　　　　$y = 6 - 30/24 - 42 = 12/9$

　　　$x = -13/9$ and $y = 12/9$ **Ans.**

Q.10. $x + 7y = 9$

　　　$4x + 6y = 7$

Solution:　　　　　　　　$x = 49 - 54/28 - 6 = -5/22$

　　　　　　　　　　　　$y = 36 - 7/28 - 6 = 29/22$

　　　$x = -5/22$ and $y = 29/22$ **Ans.**

A FEW WORDS MORE ...

Now, that you have learnt and, to some extent, practised the techniques of Vedic Maths given in this book, we would advice you to continue practising these with your friends, family members and collegues, wherever and whenever possible. The continuity of this practice will make you deft in Vedic Maths improving your speed and accuracy of solving cumbersome mathematical calculations mentally without the help of calculator, computer and even paper & pen.

This practice will not only win you laurels from your friends and others but will also help you to a great extent while appearing in competitive and academic exams where you are required to do complex calculations without the help of any calculating device and that too in a very short-time, accurately.

So keep practising and amazing your friends and others, and get rid of the fear of numbers, tables and calculations to succeed in life with confidence.